Influence: On Rhetoric and Biblical Interpretation

Brill Research Perspectives in Biblical Interpretation

Editor-in-Chief

Davina C. Lopez (*Eckerd College, USA*)

Volumes published in this Brill Research Perspective are listed at *brill.com/rpbi*

Influence: On Rhetoric and Biblical Interpretation

By

Michal Beth Dinkler

BRILL

LEIDEN | BOSTON

This paperback book edition is simultaneously published as issue 4.3 (2019) of *Brill Research Perspectives in Biblical Interpretation*, DOI:10.1163/24057657-12340017.

Library of Congress Control Number: 2021903268

Typeface for the Latin, Greek, and Cyrillic scripts: "Brill". See and download: brill.com/brill-typeface.

ISBN 978-90-04-46141-3 (paperback)
ISBN 978-90-04-46142-0 (e-book)

Printed by Printforce, United Kingdom

Contents

Influence: On Rhetoric and Biblical Interpretation

Michal Beth Dinkler
Yale University, New Haven, Connecticut, USA
mb.dinkler@yale.edu

Abstract

The influence of the Bible in human history is staggering. Biblical texts have inspired grand social advancements, intellectual inquiries, and aesthetic achievements. Yet, the Bible has also given rise to hatred, violence, and oppression—often with deadly consequences. How does the Bible exert such extraordinary influence? The short answer is rhetoric. In *Influence: On Rhetoric and Biblical Interpretation*, Michal Beth Dinkler demonstrates that, contrary to popular opinion, rhetoric is not inherently "empty" or disingenuous. Rhetoric refers to the art of persuasion. Dinkler argues that the Bible is by nature rhetorical, and that understanding the art of persuasion is therefore vital for navigating biblical literature and its interpretation. *Influence* invites readers to think critically about biblical rhetoric *and* the rhetoric of biblical interpretation, and offers a clear and compelling guide for how to do so.

Keywords

rhetoric – rhetorical studies – persuasion – influence – Hebrew Bible – New Testament – biblical interpretation – uses of the Bible

Introduction

From the international space station, astronauts capture images of an iconic gash, snaking its way across the desert of northwest Arizona. The Grand Canyon. This cavernous hole in the earth's surface, millions of years in the making, bespeaks the vast and complex influence of the Colorado River. I mean this literally; the word "influence" comes from the Medieval Latin term *influere*, "to flow into, stream in, pour in." The Grand Canyon exists because the Colorado River flowed into and coursed through the Arizona desert with such tremendous force that it carved indelible channels through layers and layers of land and limestone.

The Bible is like that raging river. For millennia, humans have made decisions based on biblical texts, in ways both collective and individual, conscious and unintentional. Obviously, this is true for Jews and Christians, whose Bibles are foundational for their respective traditions. Less obvious, perhaps, but no less true, is the fact that the Bible's influence flows beyond the borders of any single community, culture, place, time period, or civilization. The Bible's shaping force affects even those who are not adherents of any religion, because the flow of human history has been determined, at least in part, by matters of biblical interpretation.

The Bible has served as a seemingly inexhaustible source of motivation and justification for every side of every social movement. Child labor reformers, those fighting poverty, and climate justice activists have been motivated by biblical texts. But so have the Nazis, the Ku Klux Klan, and present-day white supremacists. The Bible has *in-fluenced*—poured into, carved out, forged and formed—widely diverse legal, social, and political systems. Its winding whirlpools of words have carved grand canyons of social advancement, intellectual inquiry, and aesthetic achievement. Yet, amidst these sediments, the Bible has also deposited sediments of violence, hatred, and oppression, with very real and often very deadly consequences.

What's more, time and again, the Bible's vast and complex influence has been evident on opposing sides of the *very same* issue. As Shakespeare's Antonio puts it in *The Merchant of Venice*, "Even the devil can cite scripture for his purpose" (Shakespeare 1992: I.iii.98). Consider American slavery. On December 10, 1641, the fledgling Massachusetts Bay Colony passed their first law legalizing slavery, with the horrifyingly ironic title, "Bodies of Liberty." The writers state explicitly that they will bind black bodies based on the biblical Mosaic Law:

> There shall never be any bond slavery, villenage, nor captivity among us, unless it be lawful captives, taken in just wars, and such strangers as willingly sell themselves or are sold unto us, and these shall have all the liberties and Christian usages which *the law of God established in Israel requires* …

Early American slaveholders justified their views and policies using their particular interpretations of the Holy Scriptures.

Just as evident in the sediment and schist of history are courageous counterexamples—heroic enslaved Africans and later abolitionists, for example, who based their opposition to slavery on very different understandings of the Bible. There is a long, varied, and rich tradition of African American interpreters who countered what Frederick Douglass called the "slavehold-ing religion" (Douglass 1845: 118), not by rejecting biblical texts (though some did so), but by rejecting the interpretations of biblical texts that they heard from white masters (Bowens 2020). In the nineteenth century, for instance, Peter Randolph, an emancipated slave-turned-reverend denounced preach-ers who defended slavery, likening them to Ananias and Sapphira in the book of Acts, who "betrayed the trust committed to them" (quoted in Powery and Sadler 2016: 6). Another nineteenth-century former slave, James Pennington, used New Testament texts to declare that redemption from "all iniquity" (Tit. 2:14) includes redemption from the sinful system of slavery; "the gospel rightly understood, taught, received, felt and practiced," Pennington wrote to his parents, "is anti-slavery as it is anti-sin" (quoted in Bowens 2020: 147–49). Many other forceful arguments against the dehumanization and subjuga-tion of black folks were grounded in liberative interpretations of biblical passages. In these discourses, the biblical texts themselves really matter, which means that the *rhetoric* of the texts takes center stage, whether it is recognized as rhetoric or not.

The Bible has been used on opposing sides of debates not only about slavery, but also about: orthodoxy and heresy and establishment of Christian doctrines; legitimation of and opposition to imperial expansion, war, and conquest; dis-agreements over modern science, the age of the earth, and commodification of natural resources; delineation of women's roles in various public and private spheres, and in the ranks of ordained clergy; the nature of sex, gender, and selfhood, and related social practices such as marriage. In these and countless other cases, we see the Bible's tremendous influence at work, powerfully shap-ing the worlds in which we live.

Cynics might say that believers simply use biblical texts to legitimate their choices *ex post facto*, like a belated stamp of divine approval on what were already foregone conclusions. It is true that some are morally corrupt and use biblical texts to serve their own personal agendas. Other readers are well-intentioned, but approach the Bible uncritically as an unambiguous moral guidebook; for these readers, the original authors' "pens were in the firm grip of the Holy Spirit," and the meaning of the Holy Spirit's words in Scripture is simply self-evident (Anderson and Moore 2008: 4). However, interpretive processes are complex, even if they seem intuitive to us. Still other believers recognize these complexities and wrestle carefully with difficult interpretive questions. There are many ways to read the Bible and thus, many ways to be influenced, informed, formed, and transformed by the biblical texts.

Discussions of the Bible's influence often focus on whether biblical texts *should* or *should not* impact people's lives. One extreme is represented by those who hear "Bible" and think "outdated religious text." For this camp, the Bible is nothing more than words—arbitrary marks, crowded together on ancient parchment, that are inapplicable in the modern world. According to this view, allowing the Bible to influence one's life choices today is inappropriate and, at times, damaging. The other extreme is represented by those who hear "Bible" and think "Timeless and Eternal Truth." Indeed, for billions of people around the world, the so-called "Good Book" is much more than just a "good book": it is divine revelation, God's Word. Whether the faithful invoke labels like "inerrant," "infallible," or "humanly authored but divinely inspired," they typically ascribe the Bible's authority to divine authorship. "All scripture," declared the writer of 2 Timothy, "is inspired by God and is useful for teaching, for reproof, for correction, and for training in righteousness" (2 Tim. 3:16). The belief that God uniquely communes with and communicates with humans through this singular script renders the words of the Bible anything but arbitrary. The Bible, from this perspective, *ought* to influence the hearts and minds of human beings.

Geologists do not get caught up in discussions of whether water pressure *should* or *should not* have formed the Grand Canyon. They are more concerned with *how* it did so, and where its forces may flow in the future. Similarly, this volume is not about whether the words of the Bible *should* or *should not* direct decisions or change people's choices. Whatever one might think about the Bible's origins or nature, whatever one's assessments of its readers, the starting point for this volume is the undeniable fact that the Bible *does* influence. Studying the inner workings of the Bible's staggering influence is crucial because the consequences of biblical interpretations are not abstract or hypothetical. They are real. And like a geologist who seeks to understand the Colorado River's ongoing influence on the face of the earth, the scholar who seeks to understand the Bible's ongoing influence may even have the opportunity to shape the path it carves into the face of human experience in the future.

How do the written words of Scripture exert such extraordinary influence? More broadly, how do any kinds of written words persuade, if words themselves have no will? How is it that humans can use words, and not just physical violence or coercive force, to convince one another to think or do particular things?

The very short answer, and the true topic of this very short volume, is *rhetoric*.

The Bible as (Empty) Rhetoric?

I am well aware that hearing the Bible described as "rhetorical" will make some people nervous. This is because, in popular parlance today, "rhetoric" connotes falsehood, spin, hollow promises, or propaganda. In this current era of political polarization and so-called "Fake News," a common charge against those with whom we disagree is to say that they spout "empty rhetoric." Sometimes, we simply condemn others' "rhetoric" without any qualifier at all. Usually, such a charge indicates that their words, and often their character, are untrustworthy or morally vacuous, that their claims are unreliable. A quick search on social media yields multiple posts contrasting #EmptyRhetoric with #Facts. A human rights activist working on behalf of refugees declares: "We need Refuge from Our Rhetoric." Responding to a panel on poverty in Africa, someone else tweets: "Tired of this #rhetoric. Talk is cheap." When we label something "rhetoric," we typically mean to say it is *not* the truth. Of course, such views are not new; suspicion of rhetoric stretches back to antiquity. It is easy to imagine Plato on Twitter or Instagram: *Beware*!, he might post, *Rhetoric is an #evilcraft* (*Laws* 937e).

The widespread perception that rhetoric is disingenuous clearly presents a special challenge for students of biblical literature. If rhetoric is equated with falsehood and/or malicious intent, then those who view the Bible as the inerrant, divinely-inspired Word of God will understandably be offended by any insinuation that the biblical writings are rhetorical. As this volume will show, however, conflating "rhetoric" with falsehood or propaganda reflects a fundamental misunderstanding of what rhetoric is and how it works.

Rhetoric, broadly, is *the art of persuasion*. Aristotle wrote that the ability "to see the available means of persuasion … is the function of no other art" (*Rhetorica* 1.2.1). The claim that a biblical text is "rhetorical" simply means that *it aims to influence*. Whatever else the Bible may be, it is, at base, a collection of ancient texts written by human beings in specific locations for particular reasons—one of which is indisputably to *persuade* readers to do and believe all kinds of things. Understanding the art of persuasion is therefore vital for navigating both biblical scholarship and the literature that it takes as its focus. I have written this volume of *Brill Research Perspectives in Biblical Interpretation* for professional scholars and graduate students in biblical studies who may be conversant with—and perhaps are even specialists in—*other* approaches or modes of biblical interpretation, but for whom the ongoing conversation regarding biblical rhetoric remains disorienting.

Certain biblical texts say explicitly that they mean to persuade. The Gospel of Luke begins with a clear statement of its writer's motivation: "I decided …

to write … *so that* you might know for certain the things about which you have been taught" (1:3–4).[1] The author of the Gospel of John closes his narrative by stating unequivocally that persuasion was his goal: "These things are written *so that* you might believe that Jesus is the Christ, the Son of God, and *so that* believing, you might have life in his name" (20:31). These two examples refer to "believing" (*pisteuō*) and "knowing" (*epiginōskō*), but it is important to recognize that ancient notions of persuasion are broader than Western, post-Enlightenment conceptions of "belief" or "knowledge."

For the biblical writers, persuasion meant more than inducing rational, disembodied cognitive assent. The authors of biblical texts sought to influence their audiences on multiple levels and in many ways—certainly including, but not limited to, intellectual agreement. For instance, the apostle Paul stipulates in his letter to the slaveholder Philemon that he is writing to "appeal to" or "encourage" (*parakaleō*, twice in Phlmn. 9–10) Philemon on behalf of the enslaved man, Onesimus; Paul writes to persuade Philemon not only to carry out a particular action (i.e., to "welcome" Onesimus back into his home, Phlmn. 17), but also to do so in a particular way (i.e., "voluntarily," Phlmn. 14, as "a beloved brother," Phlmn. 16). In a letter to the Christian community in Corinth, Paul explains that he writes so that his recipients will change their behavior, implying that if they do not, they will face negative consequences: "I write these things while I am away from you, *so that* when I come, I may not have to be severe" (2 Cor. 13:10). The author of the first Johannine missive is more succinct: "I write this to you *so that* you will not sin" (1 John 2:1).

These claims constitute rhetoric. Other biblical texts are less overt about their persuasive aims, but nevertheless *function* as rhetorical. The Hebrew Bible, while devoid of explicit authorial declarations regarding rhetorical purpose (Zulick 1992), contains many texts that are meant to move readers toward specific beliefs and behaviors and away from others. Deuteronomy 28:58–59, for example, issues a dire warning:

> If you do not diligently observe all the words of this law that are written in this book … then the LORD will overwhelm both you and your offspring with severe and lasting afflictions and grievous and lasting maladies.

This, too, is rhetoric. Through direct address and the promise of negative consequences should its claim on the reader be ignored, this text attempts to persuade.

---

1 Hereafter, I will refer to the biblical authors by their traditional names for the sake of convenience, without implying anything about their historical authors.

Sometimes, the persuasive nature of biblical literature is implicit, even difficult to detect. Take Exodus 32:16, for instance. The narrator states that Moses has been given a covenant, written on tablets, which "were the work of God, and the writing was the writing of God, engraved upon the tablets." *This is also rhetoric.* On the surface, it may seem to be simply a neutral descriptive detail, a straightforward representation of the covenant that Moses carries down the mountain to the people of Israel. However, the description itself serves a persuasive function: by virtue of what literary critic Roland Barthes called *l'effet de reel*, the effect of reality (Barthes 1968; see also Ankersmit 1989), the description suggests that the commandments should be uniquely binding, because the words were engraved by God. This statement of literal divine authorship is a rhetorical strategy, an implicit claim that these words are more than human carvings etched in stone. They are meant to move from the face of things—here, from the surface of stone tablets—to create deeper change in what other biblical writers describe as the "tablets of the heart" (e.g., Prov. 3:3; 7:3; 2 Cor. 3:2–3). Rhetorically, the description of the stone tablets in Exodus 32:16 is more than a straightforward representation of an unmediated reality; it is a subtle persuasive claim that the words written on the tablets ought to influence those for whom they were written, both those waiting for Moses at the base of the mountain, and those reading (and reciting) them later.

Why does any of this matter?

Biblical Rhetoric: What's at Stake

The Law of Moses, upon which American slaveholders based their first law legalizing slavery, "Bodies of Liberty," *is rhetoric*. It is an attempt to persuade that was used to persuade. Real lives hung in the balance then, and life and death continue to be at stake as the legacies of slavery reverberate in racist rhetoric today.

Slavery is not an anomaly in this regard. Anti-Judaism is another clear example. Christians today often do not realize (perhaps do not wish to realize) the extent to which New Testament rhetoric fueled the Nazis' hatred of the Jews, nor how certain formulations of Christianity continue to legitimize anti-Semitism today in their own rhetoric (Reinhartz 2018). When the author of the Gospel of Matthew writes that "all the people" at Jesus' trial shouted, "Let his blood be on us and on our children!" (Matt. 27:25), *that is rhetoric.* When the author of the Gospel of John tells us that Jesus called his Jewish interlocutors the devil's offspring (Jn. 8:44), *that is rhetoric.* These are the Gospel writers' attempts to persuade. Unfortunately, generations of readers have taken these biblical texts (and other similar passages) *not* as attempts to persuade, but as clear, complete, and impartial accounts of "what actually happened" in the past and of "how things actually are" in the present. Reading negative depictions of the Jews at face value has led countless people to conclude that the Jews *actually were* responsible for Jesus' crucifixion, and that their descendants *actually are* culpable for his death. Jews and Judaism become the embodiment of sin and evil, and Jesus becomes the Savior who frees believers from both. Moreover, many Christians extrapolate further from these conclusions that they have no choice but to denounce or (perhaps quietly) reject Jews and Judaism as anti-Christ and anti-God. In a post-Holocaust world, ignorance of the supercessionism in many Christians' biblical interpretations perpetuates violence of different kinds.

Those who *are* cognizant of the harmful legacy of certain biblical texts often struggle to know what to do with them today. Are these passages evidence of an immoral God? Do they provide reason to reject Christianity? The philosopher Bertrand Russell famously answers "yes" in his, "Why I am not a Christian":

> You will find that in the Gospels Christ said, "Ye serpents, ye generation of vipers, how can ye escape the damnation of Hell." That was said to people who did not like His preaching. It is not really to my mind quite the best tone, and there are a great many of these things about Hell.

Rejecting the Bible altogether is not the only interpretive option, however. Recognizing that biblical texts are rhetorical opens up other possibilities.

Of what, exactly, did New Testament writers intend to persuade their respective audiences with these portrayals? Did John *want* his audience to see all Jews as evil? We cannot know. Perhaps the vituperative treatments of the Jews in John's Gospel are an impassioned response to a concrete historical situation. Johannine scholars frequently posit, based on the key term *aposynagōgos* ("expelled from the synagogue," Jn. 9:22; 12:42; 16:2), that the Johannine community had been kicked out of their local synagogue for confessing Jesus as the Messiah (Martyn 2003). Did Matthew personally believe that the Jewish crowd was responsible for Jesus' crucifixion, and that Pilate only reluctantly gave the order? Again, we cannot know. Perhaps Matthew depicts the Jews as responsible for Jesus' crucifixion, and the reluctant Pilate as almost an innocent bystander, because his larger persuasive goal is to convince the Romans that followers of Jesus are not a threat to Roman rule. Explanations like these are rooted in historical reconstructions of the authors' unique contexts, and the circumstances that may have shaped their persuasive intentions.

Of course, it is also true that biblical literature is not just itself rhetorical. It has also been *used* rhetorically, often in ways that the writers themselves could never have imagined. We cannot know with complete certainty what John or

Matthew or any other biblical author intended when they depicted Jews and Judaism negatively. We can, however, observe how actual interpreters have *been persuaded by* their rhetoric, and we can recognize the dire consequences of a failure to understand them as rhetorical.

Reception history traces how biblical interpreters in scholarly, ecclesial, and popular contexts are always appropriating texts from the past as instruments of influence for their own present circumstances. The Exodus story's revolutionary liberative rhetoric, for instance, has long been used in the fight for freedom (Marbury 2015), and the book of Revelation's enigmatic apocalyptic rhetoric has repeatedly been used to manufacture predictions of the end times (O'Leary 1991).

The upshot is this: Rhetoric itself is not empty or substantive, moral or immoral, true or false. Certainly, people persuade others for nefarious reasons, toward unethical outcomes; Wayne Booth calls the manipulative use of persuasion "rhetrickery" (Booth 2004: x). But not all rhetoric is rhetrickery. People often persuade others for virtuous reasons, toward ethical outcomes (and people also disagree about the definitions of "virtuous" and "ethical"). Biblical literature is, in fact, deeply concerned with the consequences of persuasion. We find in the Bible countless depictions of persuasive acts, from the serpent in Eden persuading Eve to eat forbidden fruit (Gen. 3:1–5), to Noah surviving the flood because he was persuaded to do "all the LORD commanded him" (Gen 7:5), to the apostles persuading others of the Gospel message "to the ends of the earth" (Acts 1:8). Herein lies the tremendous power—both the blessing and the bane—of the art of persuasion: Rhetoric has the potential to move humans toward good *or* toward evil.

Biblical scholars have been working to understand this power for years.

Biblical Scholarship and Rhetorical Analysis

As far as biblical scholars are concerned, the *rhetoricity*—that is, the rhetorical nature—of biblical texts is not in question. Where debates do arise is around a multitude of seemingly basic but infinitely complex questions: Of what, exactly, were individual authors of biblical texts trying to persuade their intended audiences, and why? What kinds of rhetoric are employed toward those ends? How do biblical texts' persuasive aims and claims relate to their historical, ideological, and theological aims and claims? How do those textual characteristics relate more broadly to fact and fiction, truth and falsehood, right and wrong? Do different languages and the thought worlds they represent, such as Hebrew or Greek, persuade differently? Should interpreters refer to classical Greco-Roman rhetorical conventions when analyzing the texts of the Hebrew Bible? Do distinct genres, such as epistles or narratives, persuade differently? How can interpreters be persuaded by the very same texts of diametrically opposed positions? What difference does (or should) it make that biblical texts were written by and for people from vastly different time periods, regions, and cultures, often as far removed from each other as they are from us? What are the ethical implications of the Bible's uses of rhetoric, and of biblical scholars' and others' rhetorical claims about them? Do we always want to reproduce the rhetoric we find in biblical texts? Why or why not?

Questions like these are the purview of rhetorical analysis. Biblical scholars have engaged in rhetorical analysis for a long time, and from varying perspectives. In fact, newcomers to this area of biblical scholarship might well be deterred by the sheer number of publications related to rhetoric and biblical interpretation. To give but one example, Duane Watson's 2006 "bibliographic survey," *The Rhetoric of the New Testament*, consists of nearly 200 pages of single-spaced references, and no annotations or references to the Hebrew Bible are included (see similarly Watson and Hauser 1994). Since Watson's bibliography was published in 2006, the proliferation of related publications has given rise to what is now a truly massive body of literature about biblical rhetoric.

Not only is the number of publications about biblical rhetoric daunting, but the conceptions of rhetoric one finds therein can be frustratingly polysemous. In 1997, Dennis Stamps observed: "There is no single overarching methodology ... in the current practice of rhetorical criticism" (Stamps 1997: 223). Now, over twenty years later, Stamps's observation remains entirely à propos. Biblical scholars use the term "rhetoric" in different ways, and approach the study of rhetoric with different emphases and presuppositions. Just as someone from Ireland might struggle to understand an American's accents and intonations, though both are speaking English, it can be difficult to understand various scholars' versions of rhetorical analysis, though they use the same word, "rhetoric."

In this volume, I adopt Steven Mailloux's broad definition of rhetoric as "the political effectivity of trope and argument in culture" (Mailloux 1989: xii). Mailloux reflects on the flexibility of this definition:

> Such a working definition includes the two traditional meanings of rhetoric—figurative language and persuasive action—and permits me to emphasize either or both senses, differently in different discourse at different historical moments, in order to specify more exactly how texts affect their audiences in terms of particular power relations.
>
> MAILLOUX 1989: xii

Mailloux's goal of "specify[ing] more exactly how texts affect their audiences" is my goal with rhetorical analysis of biblical texts, as well.

We can divide the topic of textual rhetoric into three distinct categories:

1)   the *practice* of rhetoric, both *in* the text and *of* the text—including the rhetorical strategies employed by characters in stories and by implied authors of the texts themselves;

2)   discourse *about* rhetoric—including ancient instructions in rhetoric, such as the "how to" manuals (called *progymnasmata*) used in elite Greco-Roman educational contexts, and reflections on rhetoric, such as the theoretical discussions we find in Plato's *Phaedrus*;

3)   modern scholarly rhetoric critically analyzing all of the above—including biblical scholars working in the area of rhetoric, and researchers in the separate academic discipline of rhetorical studies.

These categorical distinctions can be useful heuristically, but it is important to remember that humans have been practicing, studying, and theorizing about rhetoric for millennia, and they often do so in dialogue with, responding to, and informing one another. You might think of all the texts we will discuss in this volume as partners in what Kenneth Burke famously described as the "unending conversation":

> Imagine that you enter a parlor. You come late. When you arrive, others have long preceded you, and they are engaged in a heated discussion, a discussion too heated for them to pause and tell you exactly what it is about. In fact, the discussion had already begun long before any of them got there, so that no one present is qualified to retrace for you all the steps that had gone before. You listen for a while, until you decide that you have caught the tenor of the argument; then you put in your oar. Someone answers; you answer him; another comes to your defense; another aligns himself against you, to either the embarrassment or gratification of your opponent, depending upon the quality of your ally's assistance. However, the discussion is interminable. The hour grows late, you must depart. And you do depart, with the discussion still vigorously in progress.
>
> BURKE 1941: 110–11

Each text is its own powerful voice amongst many, all participating in the "interminable" human discussion that is always at work rhetorically constituting, deconstructing, and reconfiguring human social systems and relations. This includes biblical texts, which rarely announce themselves as rhetorical, but nevertheless operate as such. Often, the most powerful—and at times, the most dangerous—speakers in the unending conversation are those who do not recognize that they have joined a discussion that "had already begun long before any of them got there," and instead presume theirs is the only voice in the room worth hearing because they speak for God.

This volume stands as one scholar's offer to "pause" and explain, so that you can "[catch] the tenor of the argument" and eventually "put your oar in." Keep in mind, though, that this also means you are reading one scholar's perspective. This is my rhetoric. Burke is right: no one can "retrace for you all the steps that" preceded us in the unending conversation on rhetoric; the account I offer is selective, and, in keeping with the emphasis of the series, *perspectival.* It is unavoidably shaped by where I stand in the parlor. As an American biblical scholar working in the United States, my perspective is skewed toward Western Anglophone discourses on rhetoric, even as I try to attend to global conversations about these topics.

My rhetoric is also shaped by my own deep and abiding interest in literature as communication. What this means for this volume, practically, is that the discussion will gravitate toward the literary, textual aspects of biblical rhetoric. This is not to say that rhetoric is limited to the linguistic. Persuasion exceeds and sometimes flouts language; just think of how easily we are swayed by a smell or taste that evokes some memory or feeling, or how powerfully motivated we are by emotions, sensations, and desires we cannot always articulate. In the wake of the twentieth century's linguistic turn, many scholars of rhetoric have rightly challenged the discipline's traditional logocentrism, pushing the study of rhetoric beyond spoken and written words to consider also nonliterary, nonlinguistic forms of persuasion. Even a cursory glance at recent publications in rhetorical studies reveals no shortage of new subdisciplines that have appropriated the label "rhetoric": material rhetoric, kinesthetic rhetoric, visual and spatial rhetoric, the rhetoric of everyday life, among others. These forms of rhetoric are woven into the fabric of biblical literature, as well, though they are not the main focus of this volume.

My interests in literature and language also lead me to bracket out philosophical and theological discussions of biblical rhetoric. All rivers have tributaries, and sometimes multiple streams as outcroppings deflect the flow of water. This is true of the biblical influence, as well. We cannot follow all of these at once. Still, it is worth mentioning a few briefly, in part to indicate how I will delimit an already unwieldy topic, and in part to signal that there is far more to biblical rhetoric than I could ever hope to cover in a volume such as this.

Biblical Rhetoric and What This Volume Is Not About

Scholars have posed important philosophical and theological questions about the role of persuasion and influence in the Bible. *Theodicy*, which attempts to explain the existence of evil, might pose the question in terms of influence: If God is good, and God is omnipotent, then how should we understand God's willingness to allow evil agents (like Satan or the demons in the Gospels) to influence humans? What about God's refusal to exert divine influence in moments of tragedy—what Nicholas Wolterstorff frames as "the silence of the God who speaks" (2002: 215)? A paradigmatic biblical example is the book of Job, where Satan ("the Accuser") persuades God to give him nearly total influence over the eponymous character's life. Satan uses this power, notably gained through persuasive means, to cause Job to suffer in nearly every conceivable way. Job, despondent at God's apparent disinterest in his misery, desperately laments "Even when I cry out, 'Violence!' I am not answered; I call aloud, but there is no justice" (Job 19:7). In the Gospels of Mark and Matthew, Jesus' climactic "cry of dereliction" on the cross, "My God, my God, why have you forsaken me?" (Mk. 15:34; Matt. 27:46), points similarly to God's refusal to intervene and influence Jesus' executioners toward a just outcome.

Theologians also ask how human free will and divine determinism manifest in and through language. *Hamartiology*, the study of sin, includes questions about who or what influences humans toward ungodliness. Does the doctrine of original sin mean that humans have no choice but to sin, as the medieval theologian Bernard of Clairvaux teaches in his influential *On Grace and Free Choice* (e.g., vii.23)? Do demonic agents persuade humans to sin? Patristic authors in particular considered Satan "the arch-persuader at work behind the scenes in the Garden" (Jager 1993: 108), while defendants of Christian orthodoxy have frequently condemned their opponents as heretics who use "devil's rhetoric" (Calfhill 1565: fol. 172a). Does the Reformers' doctrine of predestination make God responsible for human sin? The nineteenth-century preacher Wilbur Fisk argued that it did, and denounced Calvinists for believing that God decided "to introduce sin, and influence men to commit sin, and harden them in it, that they might be the fit subjects of his wrath." Predestination, Fisk declared, "is enough to chill one's blood," for it turns God into an "Almighty Tyrant!" (Fisk 1831: 25).

Are so-called "open theists" correct that God can be influenced by human words, as when Abraham persuades God not to annihilate Sodom and Gomorrah (Gen. 18:22–33), or when Moses convinces God not to destroy the people of Israel (Exod. 32:14)? While many Christians are uncomfortable with the notion that humans can influence God, direct rhetorical address to God is a cherished feature of Jewish tradition. As Davida Charney notes, "The greatest figures of the Hebrew Bible, including Abraham, Moses, Jeremiah, and Job, are celebrated for arguing—not so much with other people, but with God" (2014: 1). The Psalms, too, as a genre of prayers, seek specifically and repeatedly to persuade God. The Psalmist, for instance, implores: "Grant me justice Lord, as befits my righteousness" (Ps. 7:8); "Save me from the wrongdoers, and from men of bloodshed rescue me" (Ps. 59:2); "Have regard for the covenant ... do not let the downtrodden be put to shame" (Ps. 74:20–21). Charney argues that such efforts to persuade God are undergirded by a theological assumption that "God's willingness to argue rather than just lay down the law bespeaks an extraordinary generosity toward humanity" (2014: 2).

Relatedly, theologians have asked whether otherworldly and/or miraculous language differs ontologically from human language. Is God's language more persuasive than human language simply by virtue of its all-powerful source? On the one hand, Genesis 1–2 portrays God's speech as so powerfully generative that the entire creation is spoken into existence; texts like Jeremiah 20:7–9 declare that God's speech is overwhelming and impossible to resist. Indeed, throughout biblical literature, God, God's emissaries, and God's enemies are portrayed repeatedly and powerfully influencing human characters through their speech, and human responses to them are at times depicted through struggles over speech regulation (e.g., Gen. 11:1–9; Exod. 4:10–16; Lk. 1:5–65). On the other hand, the entire prophetic tradition is predicated on the fact that people are unpersuaded by God's words: humans consistently resist, disobey, and ignore divine commands. Human and supernatural language are tangled up together in complicated ways when God and demons speak through humans (e.g., Micah 6:1; Mk. 5:6–9), and in passages about charisms like glossolalia or the miraculous comprehension of languages without translation (e.g., 1 Cor. 14; Acts 2; 10:46; 19:6).

Some scholars ask how the sacrality of Scripture's rhetoric relates to persuasion. Does the Bible reveal the holy, or is the writing itself in some sense holy? Lynn Poland, drawing on Rudolf Otto's notion of the *mysterium tremendum* (Otto called it *schauervolles Geheimnis*, or "terrible mystery"), describes the Bible's language as a "peculiar rhetoric of sublimity" (Poland 1990: 30). The peculiarity of the Bible's rhetoric is theologically significant in a different way for Walter Brueggemann, who argues that:

> ... the theology of the Old Testament does not trade in a set of normative ideas that may be said in many ways, but in a peculiar utterance that is spoken and/or written in a certain way.... In terms of theological

> interpretation, because the *what* is linked to the *how*, one cannot general-
> ize or summarize but must pay attention to the detail.
>
>   BRUEGGEMANN 1997: 55; see, similarly, Brueggemann's students Linafelt and
>   Beal 1998

For these interpreters, the rhetoric of biblical texts (the "how" of what is
written) proves revelatory, not only with respect to the human authors' constructions of the language, but also—and most significantly—with respect to
God's nature.

   As valuable as these theological and philosophical discussions are, I follow a
different stream: I focus in this volume on the dynamics of persuasion between
humans and texts, rather than the nature of persuasion between humans and
demonic or divine agents. At the same time, we should never lose sight of the
crucial added valence that in biblical texts, human acts of persuasion tend
to be cloaked in or accompanied by claims about the divine. When biblical
claims and their interpretations are linked to or constitute claims about who
God is and what God wants, the stakes become exceedingly high.

   It is precisely because the stakes are so high that we cannot afford to ignore
the biblical texts' rhetoricity. I agree with David Jasper that "at the heart of
religious rhetoric, quite distinctively, lies authoritative proclamation," and,
more pressingly, that "the consequences of this absolute, rhetorical demand
have not been properly recognized" (Jasper 1990: 136). I would go so far as to
say that it is the *failure to recognize the rhetoricity of biblical texts* that leads
so many readers to reproduce biblical rhetoric toward violent ends, as when
people uncritically but authoritatively mimic Levitical rhetoric that calls for
the death of men who "lie with" men, or the Gospel rhetoric discussed above
that depicts Jews as hypocrites and Christ killers (e.g., Lev. 20:13; Matt. 27:25).
More often than not, these readers approach the Bible with good intentions;
they desire to lead biblically-informed, God-honoring lives, and to influence
others toward behavior they believe is good and right. Unfortunately, even the
best of intentions cannot keep us from inflicting harm through problematic
rhetorical uses of biblical texts. Studying rhetoric is one way to guard against
this powerful tendency.

   The volume has three major parts: Part 1, "Rhetoric: What It Is (And Isn't),
and How It Has Been Studied," explores more deeply several of the foundational issues mentioned already, such as debates about the definition of rhetoric, and introduces major moments in the study of rhetoric. Part 2, "Approaches
to Biblical Rhetoric," describes how modern biblical scholars have engaged
with and employed varying forms of rhetorical criticism to illuminate not
only biblical texts, but also the scholarship we produce about them. Because

the study of biblical rhetoric has evolved differently in critical scholarship about the Hebrew Bible and the New Testament, I make special note of parallels and divergences between the subfields. Part 3, "Reading the Rhetorics of First Peter," demonstrates the benefits of various approaches to rhetorical interpretation by analyzing the First Epistle of Peter as an example of Jewish apocalyptic rhetoric about suffering.

My own rhetorical goals are these: By the end of this volume, I will have succeeded if you are persuaded that biblical texts are fundamentally rhetorical; that we ought to be paying careful sustained attention to the rhetoric of biblical texts *and* to the rhetoric we use when thinking and talking about them; and that you have the necessary conceptual tools and resources to start analyzing the rhetoric of texts yourself.

Like those who saw the first iconic images of the Grand Canyon from space, our initial question must be: What exactly are we looking at here?

1   Rhetoric: What It Is (and Isn't) and How It Has Been Studied

1.1   *Defining Rhetoric*

The term "rhetoric" has become so unwieldy over time that it is nearly impossible to define. Typically, "rhetoric" is associated with the systematic, reasoned oratorical methods by which a successful *rhētor* persuades an audience. "Rhetoric," in this case, refers to an ancient technical art (Greek, *technē*; Latin *ars*), discussed as far back as Plato's Socrates (*Phaedrus*, 261a), and developed most fully by Greco-Roman orators like Cicero and Quintilian (about whom I will say more below). Cicero, for his part, defines rhetoric as "speech designed to persuade" (*dicere ad persuadendum accommodate*, De Or. 1.31.138). Over a century later, Quintilian, after analyzing previous definitions of rhetoric for an entire chapter, finally omits "persuasion" and opts for the more ambiguous definition of *rhetorice* as "the art of speaking well" (*ars bene dicendi*, *Inst. Or.* 2.17.37). He further divides *rhetorice* into three categories: the ability (*bene dicendi scientia*, "knowing how to speak well"), the actor (*orator*, "the orator"), and the result of the ability enacted (*bona oratio*, "good oratory") (*Inst. Or.* 2.14).

Following the major intellectual shifts occasioned by modernity (also discussed below), scholars began to develop more expansive definitions of rhetoric. The term came to be used for practice, process, *and* product. In the mid-twentieth century, Burke defined rhetoric as "the use of words by human agents to form attitudes or to induce actions in other human agents" (1953: 41), and later wrote that "wherever there is meaning, there is 'persuasion'" (1969: 172). John Bender and David Wellbery, drawing together practice and theory, propose the term "rhetoricality" to refer to "the underlying features both of modern [rhetorical] practice and of the theories that seek to account for it" (Bender and Wellberry 1990: 26). Conceptions of rhetoric expanded even more when, by the turn of the last century, theorists began to insist that words are not the only means of influencing others; wordless communication is also persuasive. Consider Kevin DeLuca's definition of rhetoric as "the mobilization of signs for the articulation of identities, ideologies, consciousnesses, communities, publics, and cultures" (DeLuca 1999: 17). DeLuca does not stipulate what kinds of "signs" are mobilized—verbal, visual, tangible, or otherwise. Some scholars, such as Terry Eagleton, use "rhetoric" to refer to every act of message-sharing, whether general or specific, verbal or nonverbal in form (Eagleton 1983: 194). For Eagleton and others, then, rhetoric becomes a metalabel for all human communication. Others critique rhetoric's traditional anthropomorphism, insisting that human communication is conditioned by extrahuman environmental factors, and that nonhumans also communicate rhetorically (e.g., Luhmann 1989).

Extremely broad conceptions of rhetoric make some scholars worry that the term will become so diffuse as to delimit nothing in particular. Booth, for one, wonders whether the ambiguity of rhetoric "muddies the distinction between the art of rhetoric and the study of the art. The practice of rhetoric is not the same as the systematic effort to study and improve that practice" (2009: 9). In a sense, such worries are justified. As an academic discipline, the study of rhetoric is amorphous, and its boundaries, porous. Scholars of rhetoric draw constantly from other interpretation-related disciplines, like hermeneutics, reader-response and reception theories, and they cross over into movements such as feminism, postcolonialism, political and cultural studies; in biblical studies, rhetoric crosses over into theology and religion (among others). Disciplinary and conceptual overlaps like these can make it difficult to demarcate how or whether rhetoric differs from other discursive forms. Sometimes, one meaning of "rhetoric" morphs imperceptibly and without warning into another.

But rhetoric has always been capricious. Even in antiquity, rhetoric-related terms were malleable. Classicist Richard Buxton, for example, observes that in Gorgias's *Encomion of Helen*, the word *peitho* (typically translated into English as "persuasion") is used as an abstract noun *and* as a proper name for the mythical goddess *Peithō*:

> For Gorgias, *peitho* is the instrument used by every speaker in ordinary contexts. Yet it is also a quasi-divine force ... *peitho* is the seductive persuasion which may have been what induced Helen to go off with Paris.

> Yet it is also the power used and the effect produced by oratory in contexts which we would regard as non-erotic.
>
> BUXTON 1982: 31

Ancient deliberations over how one ought to translate the Greek *rhētorikē* into Latin reflect these ambiguities of meaning. In *Institutes* 2.14, Quintilian ultimately finds no suitable term and so simply transliterates the Greek (i.e., *rhetorice*). Discussions of rhetoric have always been shaped by contestation over its meaning.

Conceptual capaciousness does not have to become what Walker and Benson describe as "an incoherent miscellaneousness" (Walker and Benson 2012: 2). I consider Booth's worries about muddying the waters with broad definitions of rhetoric *not* as a mandate to abandon broad definitions altogether, but as a salient reminder that precise explanations and qualifications are necessary. In fact, these terminological concerns speak to the very need for rhetoric, insofar as rhetoric functions—to use yet another twentieth-century definition—as "the art of removing misunderstanding" (Richards 1936: 11).

Modern scholars of rhetoric have attempted to remove misunderstanding in a number of ways. Rhetoric is commonly subdivided using *temporal* qualifiers, such as "classical rhetoric" or "medieval rhetoric"; *personal* qualifiers like "Burkean rhetoric"; or *categorical* qualifiers, as in "political rhetoric," "feminist rhetoric," or "apocalyptic rhetoric." Some writers distinguish between "rhetoric" (singular) and "rhetorics" (plural) (Pire 1980); the former refers to the classical, technical Greco-Roman discipline described above, while the latter refers to specialized or localized ways of thinking and speaking that are unique to specific locations or communities (e.g., "rhetorics of knowledge").[2]

In short, the bottom line is that there is no uniform definition of rhetoric. Patricia Bizzell and Bruce Herzberg offer sage advice:

> Rhetoric is a complex discipline with a long history: It is less helpful to try to define it once and for all than to look at the many definitions it has accumulated over the years and to attempt to understand how each arose and how each still inhabits and shapes the field.
>
> BIZZELL and HERZBERG 2001: 1

---

2   This singular/plural differentiation often corresponds with other contemporary distinctions. For example, the canons of classical "rhetoric" (singular) are discussed as an ancient set of *pre*scriptive rules for composition, while localized "rhetorics" are cast as *de*scriptive, not *pre*scriptive. Another way to say this is that rhetoric refers to practice, while rhetorics refers to theory. Modern American institutions of higher education perpetuate related dichotomies, housing the study of ancient rhetoric in Classics departments, and studies of rhetorics and rhetorical practices in Literature, Writing, Marketing, and/or Communication departments.

The following section takes up Bizzell and Herzberg's suggestion, keeping multiple definitions of rhetoric in play as we "attempt to understand how each arose and how each still inhabits and shapes the field[s]" of rhetorical studies first, and then, of the various subdisciplines within biblical studies.

1.2   *Studying Rhetoric*

1.2.1   The Study of Rhetoric: Two Major Moments

Rhetorical studies is an exciting and ever-changing modern field of scholarly inquiry, but its roots are ancient. Keeping in mind Burke's point that it would be impossible to recount the entire history of rhetorical studies as a discipline, this section provides a way into the discussion by describing two watershed phases in the study of rhetoric: formalizations of classical rhetoric in antiquity, and the development of modern rhetorical studies in the twentieth century. Each played a pivotal role in the rhetorical theorizing of its era, and each continues to have lasting effects in current discussions of rhetoric's remarkable power.

After introducing these two major moments in the study of rhetoric, I shall discuss the various ways that biblical scholars have appropriated and applied them in the study of biblical literature.

1.2.1.1   *Classical Rhetoric*

"Classical rhetoric" refers to the formalized technical art of persuasion. This rhetoric "as *technē*" is typically traced back to so-called "Sophists" like Protagoras and Gorgias in the fifth century BCE. Cicero (*Brutus* 44) and others later credited two Sicilians, Corax and Tisias (possibly the same person), with the invention of rhetoric, mentioning the need to litigate property rights following the rise of Athenian democracy. Of course, rhetorical *practice* did not begin with the Sophists or the Sicilians; practices of persuasion are clearly evident in earlier Homeric literature, for example. As Pseudo-Plutarch put it in the second century CE, "No reasonable person will deny that Homer was an artificer of discourse (*technitēs logōn*)" (*Essay on the Life and Poetry of Homer* 171). And notions of persuasion, power, influence, and language were linked already in archaic Greece, as evidenced not least by worship of Peithō (see, e.g., Hesiod's *Works and Days* 73; Aristophanes's *Lysistrata* 202–4).

Though the systematization of rhetoric is conventionally attributed to the Sophists, it was truly codified by citizens of Athenian democracy in the fourth century BCE. When democracy was first introduced in Athens, citizens would appear before an assembly and attempt to convince others to vote freely for or against a given agenda. With the rise of the new political system, rhetorical competence became requisite for the welfare of society and its citizens: "To be political, to live in a polis, meant that everything was decided through words and persuasion and not through force and violence" (Arendt 1958: 26–27). These ancient roots attest to rhetoric's longstanding role in legal and civic discourse, and explain why some still define rhetoric as "persuasive *public* discourse" (Andrews: 1983: 4, emphasis added). Indeed, rhetoric has always held a privileged place in the public square.

As the need for skilled orators rose for the Athenians, so did the need for intentional systematized training in rhetoric. Extant treatises and handbooks of the preliminary exercises used in ancient rhetorical education (progymnasmata), in conjunction with legal addresses, panegyric speeches, and oratorical compositions, paint a fairly clear picture of the schools and itinerant tutors who offered specialized instruction to elite young males in the "science of speaking well" (*bene dicendi Scientia*; see, e.g., Loo and Livingstone 1998).[3] The institutionalization of rhetoric as the ground of ancient education played a crucial role in constructing and maintaining the privileges of the already propertied and powerful; for instance, advice about rhetorical delivery denounced gestures that might make one appear like uncultured "stage actors" or "day laborers" (*Rhetorica ad Herennium* 11.3.184). Rhetorical practices signified, undergirded, and upheld the uppermost stratum of ancient hierarchical society.

Unsurprisingly, then, the majority of our evidence regarding ancient rhetoric was written by and for wealthy males. Modern historians have worked hard to uncover the rhetorical activities of women in antiquity (e.g., Glenn 1997). Some ancient authors, like the Latin poet Ovid and the historian Herodotus, portray women making persuasive speeches, and a handful of women spoke authoritatively in their capacity as rulers, like the queen Cleopatra in Egypt or the Jewish queen Esther (on the rhetoric of the latter, see Muyimbu and Wénin 2017). Two female poets stand out as exemplary: the Greek Sappho, from the early sixth century BCE, and the Roman Sulpicia, from the late first century CE (on Sappho, see duBois 1995; on Sulpicia, see Flaschenriem 2005). We also have a stunning first-person account of the imprisonment and martyrdom of the Christian Saint Perpetua in the third century CE, the *Passion of Perpetua* (on the rhetoric of the latter, see Ronsse 2006). Unfortunately, we have no examples of writings about rhetoric written by women, or of women studying and practicing rhetoric in the political assemblies of ancient Greece or Rome.

The earliest systematic treatise on rhetoric, Aristotle's *Ars Rhetorica*, appears to have been written over the course of several years in the middle of the

---

3   Secondary literature on these works is extensive. Helpful surveys include Lausberg 1960; Kennedy 1994; Porter 2001; and Cribiore 2001.

fourth century BCE, and was based on lectures Aristotle delivered to his pupils. It was not published, however, until the first century CE. Though the *Ars Rhetorica* appeared relatively late in the rise of classical rhetoric, its influence throughout the centuries cannot be overstated. Still today, oratorical professions like law, along with newer fields like advertising and marketing, regularly draw on the rhetorical conventions outlined by Aristotle. Students of rhetoric learn concepts and principles from Aristotle's writings regarding all aspects of the communication triad (i.e., messenger, message, and recipient), and the three Aristotelian *pisteis*, or forms of persuasion, remain standard curricular fare (listed here with their most common English translations): *logos* (reason), *pathos* (emotion), and *ethos* (character/trustworthiness of the rhetor). Also familiar to contemporary students of rhetoric will be the three main species (*eidē*), or genres, of rhetoric, each of which Aristotle associates with specific locations and time periods (outlined in *Ars Rhet.* 1.3):

1) *judicial* rhetoric, language to accuse or defend, belongs in law courts, and concerns the past;

2) *deliberative* rhetoric, language to exhort or dissuade, belongs in assemblies of free men, and concerns the future;

3) *epideictic* rhetoric, language to praise or blame, belongs in ceremonial settings (such as memorials), and concerns the present.

In actual practice in antiquity, these rhetorical categories were utilized regularly in other arenas such as bathhouses, households, and religious assemblies, but such were the conventional Aristotelian guidelines.

In the first centuries of the Common Era, as the influence of Hellenism continued to expand throughout the Roman Empire, the arts of philosophy and rhetoric enjoyed a resurgence. It was during this period, known as the Second Sophistic, that the classic rhetorical treatises were composed to which all subsequent rhetorical training would be indebted: *De Inventione* (84 BCE) and *De Oratore* (55 BCE), both by the Roman statesman Cicero, and the twelve-volume textbook, *Institutio Oratoria* (c. 95 CE), by Cicero's great admirer, Quintilian.[4]

Both Cicero and Quintilian provide detailed instruction on rhetorical matters that had already become conventional by the time of the Second Sophistic, including the five canons of rhetoric, employed in the development of any rhetorical speech, no matter the species:

1) *inventio* (invention): developing and refining the ideas, or content, of your argument;

2) *dispositio* (arrangement, or structure): organizing the structure of your argument;

---

4 A helpful introduction remains Kennedy 1972.

3)   *elocutio* (style): improving the aesthetic style of your argument with liter-
      ary devices such as hyperbole, exempla, and figures of speech;

4)   *memoria* (memory): committing your speech to memory, as well as
      memorizing other relevant references in case you need to deliver an
      impromptu speech; and

5)   *actio* (delivery): practicing the delivery of your speech, including intona-
      tion, expression, gestures, and pronunciation.[5]

In addition to classical rules of oratory, ancient rhetoricians wrote about the
proper uses and purposes of persuasive speech. For many ancient writers, the
purpose of persuasion is to improve society by transforming listeners into better humans. Rhetoric thus played a pivotal role in ancient *psychagogy*, or the
leading of the soul toward that which is good and away from that which is evil.[6]
In the *Phaedrus*, Plato has Socrates define rhetoric as the art of "leading the
soul through words" (*Phaed.* 261A), and he later reiterates that "the function
of speech is to lead souls by persuasion" (*Phaed.* 271D). The view that words
can persuade a person to imitate virtues and eschew vices appears in ancient
literature from different time periods, geographical locations, and traditions.
Ancient thinkers as diverse as the Roman Stoic philosopher Epictetus, the
Hellenistic Jewish writer Philo, and the later Christian leader Clement of
Alexandria, all marveled at rhetoric's therapeutic power.[7]

   Though ancient writers differed in their understandings of the mechan-
ics of intellectual and affective responses, they tend to agree that persuasion
includes far more than cognitive assent (Selby 2016), and that intellect and
emotions are inextricably intertwined in the processes of persuasion. David
Konstan summarizes the ancient Greek perspective:

> The Greeks did not conceive of emotions as internal states of excitation.
> Rather, the emotions are elicited by our interpretation of the words, acts,
> and intentions of others, each in its characteristic way ... it is possible
> to alter peoples' emotions by changing their way of construing the pre-
> cipitating event.... For the Greeks, *persuasion was central to the idea of an
> emotion ...*
>
> KONSTAN 2006: xii

---

5   For a summary of these rhetorical canons in New Testament studies, see Mack 1990: 25–48.
6   Key secondary works on ancient psychagogy include Rabbow 1954; Hadot 1969; Nussbaum
    1986; Nussbaum 1994; and Dillon 1997. On psychagogy in late antiquity, see Kolbet 2010 and
    Rylaardsam 2014.
7   See, *inter alia*, Epictetus, *Discourse* 3.21.18–24; Philo, *Congr*; Clement of Alexandria, *Paed.* 43.2.

Aristotle privileged rational *logos* as the best mode of persuasion, but he also recognized the power of *non*rational influence:

> [Emotion is] all those things on account of which people *change and differ in regard to their judgments*, and upon which attend pain and pleasure, for example, anger, pity, fear, and all other such things and their opposites.
>
> *Rhet.* 2.1, 1378a20–3; emphasis added[8]

Stoicism, a branch of Hellenistic philosophy that was popular around the third century BCE, famously commended *apatheia* (passionlessness). This is often mistaken as a call to erase or avoid *pathē*, as though the Stoics considered the emotions irrelevant to persuasion, but actually, they called for the *hegemonikon* (the rational part of the soul) to control the *pathē* because they recognized the passions' enormous influential power (e.g., Seneca, *Ira* 2–3).

Rhetoric's transformative potency is one reason that opinions about the powers of rhetoric have always spanned a wide spectrum, from extremely positive to extremely negative. The disagreement turns on whether rhetoric is art or artifice. On the one hand, some see rhetoric as an art form, and rhetorical prowess as evidence of intellectual rigor, depth, and acuity. One of the most influential Athenian orators, Isocrates, unequivocally extols the merits of those who are "rhetorical":

> We regard speaking well to be the clearest sign of a good mind, which it requires, and truthful, lawful, and just speech we consider the image of a good and faithful soul.... If one must summarize the power of discourse, we will discover that nothing done prudently occurs without speech, that speech is the leader of all thoughts and actions, and that the most intelligent people use it most of all.
>
> *Nicocles* 6–7

Because rhetoric formed the foundation of a classical education in antiquity, and because education was the province of elite educated males, many, like Isocrates, associated rhetorical skill with respectability, reliability, and powerful social standing.[9]

---

8 Cf. *Nicomachean Ethics* 1105b21ff; *On the Soul* 1.1, 403a.
9 Standard texts on rhetorical education in antiquity remain Marrou 1948, Clark 1957, and Bonner 1977.

And yet, if rhetoric can change the essence of a self, then it is also potentially highly perilous. Plato portrays Socrates disparaging rhetoric by pointing out that it can be used to prey on those who lack knowledge:

> There is no need for rhetoric to know the facts at all, for it has hit upon a means of persuasion that enables it to appear in the eyes of the ignorant to know more than those who really know.
>
> *Gorgias* 459

Socrates is concerned here with those who are uneducated. However, rhetoric is not only dangerous to the gullible. If, as Isocrates puts it, "speech is the leader of all thoughts and actions," but access to such persuasive speech is limited to a privileged few, then rhetoric can serve to uphold and justify the thoughts and actions of those already in power. Systems of domination are thereby built on the passive acceptance by the many of the self-serving rhetoric of a few.

Those who equate rhetoric with artifice see a parallel with sophistry, the calculated language of one who intends to deceive. The Sophists themselves left a long and checkered legacy. It is significant that early Sophists like Antiphon and Protagoras did not form an organization or association; they were itinerant teachers who travelled from *polis* to *polis* throughout ancient Greece to train wealthy male students in philosophy and rhetoric for a fee. Ancient polemicists imputed malicious motives to skilled rhetoricians, seeing them as merely traveling charlatans—eloquent and clever, perhaps, but treacherous and self-serving, interested only in their own advancement. Both Plato and Aristotle denounced Sophists for devising fallacious arguments and caring nothing for truth. In the *Phaedrus*, for example, Plato complains that the rhetoricians Tisias and Gorgias mislead others because they "make small things seem great and great things small by the power of their words, and new things old and old things the reverse" (267a–b). Aristotle, though an avid advocate of rhetoric properly practiced, condemned rhetorical sophistry—Booth's "rhetrickery"—and held that in the best possible political system, rhetoric would be unnecessary.

Classical rhetoric took on a new face with the rise of Christianity in the Common Era. Indeed, classical rhetoric has been a central aspect of Christianity from its inception, as Christians made conspicuous use of technical rhetorical strategies to influence others toward Christian conversion. The earliest Jesus followers' uses of classical rhetoric, found in the literature of the New Testament, will be discussed below. In late antiquity, classical rhetorical conventions appear even more prominently in the Greek writings of Church leaders like John Chrysostom, Gregory of Nazianzus, and Gregory of Nyssa, and in the Latin *apologia* of former professional rhetoricians like Tertullian and Lactantius. Augustine, who was classically trained as a rhetorician, rejected biblical texts prior to his conversion "on account of their unrefined style" (*Con.* 3.5.9). After becoming a Christian, he changed his mind, extolling the rhetorical beauty of biblical literature and marshalling rhetorical theory for his own Christian apologetic purposes most famously in his *De Doctrina Christiana*. The celebrated homiletician John Chrysostom, called "Golden Mouth" for his eloquence, applied the rhetorical tools he learned from the Sophist Libanius in his preaching, even as he disavowed "pagan" sophistry. Throughout medieval times, commonly but falsely perceived as rhetoric's Dark Ages, writers such as the twelfth-century bishop John of Salisbury produced lengthy treatises, in which they "ordere[ed] and harnass[ed] a knowledge of the secular arts in the direction of Christian living and Christian scriptures" (Ward 2019: 87; see examples in Miller et al. 1973).

Classical rhetoric continued to be influential in religion, politics, education, and literature throughout the Renaissance, early Modern, and Enlightenment periods. Skipping over thousands of years in what is admittedly but necessarily a reductionistic move, we fast forward now to the rise of modern rhetorical studies.

1.2.1.2   *Modern Rhetorical Studies*

Twentieth-century rhetorical studies was marked by a "return of rhetorical inquiry, a resurgence of intellectual interest in the issues treated by classical and postclassical theoreticians of rhetoric" (Bender and Wellbery 1990: 4). Even as they sought to recover and reassess the deliberations of classical rhetorical theorists, modern scholars pushed beyond traditional boundaries, insisting that the study of persuasion should not be limited to the circumscribed aegis of ancient rhetors or later scholars trained in the formal classical tradition. Modern rhetorical studies represents a renaissance of sorts, as critics began to embrace enlarged conceptions of rhetoric.

Modern theorists (re)cast rhetoric as a feature of all language that is foundational to and necessary for humans' (co-)existence. Burke explains:

> [R]hetoric as such is not rooted in any past condition of human society. It is rooted in *an essential function of language* itself, a function that is wholly realistic, and is continually born anew; the use of language as a symbolic means of inducing cooperation in beings that *by nature* respond to symbols.
>
> BURKE 1969: 43; emphases added

Rhetoric is, in a word, inescapable. Language is *essentially* rhetorical, and humans respond *naturally* to it. These expanded conceptions of rhetoric gained broad momentum around the middle of the twentieth century, and continue to shape rhetorical scholarship in myriad ways today.

Rhetoric's modern expansion was due, in part, to concomitant developments in the fields of linguistics and philosophy. Linguists like Ferdinand de Saussure and Charles Sanders Peirce, philosophers of language like Ludwig Wittgenstein and Susanne Langer, and speech act theorists like J. L. Austin and John Searle, all drew attention to the communicative nature of signs and symbols. Using different vocabulary and approaching the topic from different angles, these thinkers all insisted that meaning is not a singular abstraction that language somehow reflects in a straightforward manner; meaning is, rather, constructed and transmitted through language, which is itself a complex underlying system of socially-determined signs and symbols.

Advancements in theories of language entered rhetorical studies in a number of ways. In 1958, French philosophers Chaim Perelman and Lucie Olbrechts-Tyteca published their influential volume, *La Nouvelle Rhétorique: Traité l'argumentation* (translated into English in 1969 as *The New Rhetoric: A Treatise on Argumentation*). Reinvigorating the classical emphasis on argumentation, *The New Rhetoric* defines an effective argument as:

> ... one which succeeds in increasing [the] intensity of adherence among those who hear it in such a way as to set in motion the intended action (a positive action or an abstention from action) or at least in creating in the hearers a willingness to act which will appear right at the moment.
>
> PERELMAN and OLBRECHTS-TYTECA 1969: 45

Perelman and Olbrechts-Tyteca's claim that successful rhetoric sets an intended action in motion gestures toward a core assumption of the modern approach that came to be called, after their book, the New Rhetoric: namely, rhetoric does not merely reflect a given audience's current circumstances; it also generates new realities.

One of the most well-known twentieth-century scholars of rhetoric is Lloyd Bitzer, whose famous notion of the *rhetorical situation* depends on the premise that rhetoric changes reality. In his 1968 article, "The Rhetorical Situation," Bitzer defines rhetoric as "a mode of *altering* reality ... by the creation of discourse which *changes* reality through the mediation of thought and action" (Bitzer 1968: 4). According to Bitzer, every rhetorical situation has three constitutive aspects: 1) *exigence*, or "an imperfection marked by urgency," that the discourse seeks to address; 2) *rhetorical audience*, or those "capable of being influenced by discourse and of being mediators of change"; and 3) *constraints*, or those "persons, events, objects, and relations" with the "power to constrain decision and action" (i.e., limit the available strategies) in response to the exigence (Bitzer 1968: 5–7). Bitzer's article has been influential but controversial. Almost immediately after its publication, critics challenged Bitzer's positivist conception of the reality "behind" a rhetorical situation, insisting that rhetorical discourse often responds not to an *actual* exigence, but to the *perception* of one.

Reader-response critics, poststructuralists, and others who contributed to the twentieth century's linguistic turn also help us to see how Bitzer's rhetorical situation is further complicated when reading rhetoric from the past, since ancient *textual* rhetoric is not delivered and received in "real time" in the same way that *spoken* rhetoric is typically delivered and received. Moreover, a text's intended rhetorical audience often differs from its actual audience, and the constraints perceived by an author may not exist or may have shifted in a text's various contexts of reception. Put simply, an author's own rhetorical situation does not always match that of a text's receiving audience (intended or otherwise). Thus, with respect to rhetorical texts from the past, such as those we find in the Bible, the three elements of the rhetorical situation are all multi-layered.

Perhaps the most pressing point to underscore from debates over Bitzer's formulation is that while rhetoric can arise from perceptions, it does not *only* operate in the world of perception. As Booth puts it, rhetoric is:

> ... the entire range of resources that human beings share for *producing effects* on one another: effects ethical (including everything about character), practical (including political), emotional (including aesthetic), and intellectual (including every academic field).
>
> BOOTH 2004: xi; emphasis added

Rhetoric does not function only in an immaterial world of the mind; it can produce actual, real-world effects and address actual, real-world issues.

Another key principle of modern rhetorical studies is that rhetoric is not solely or predominately governed by the intentions of the rhetor. If "argumentation aims at securing the adherence of those to whom it is addressed," then it must be, "in its entirety, *relative to the audience* to be influenced" (Perelman and Olbrechts-Tyteca 1969: 19; emphasis added). Rhetoric's functions and effects are determined in and by specific communities, which are themselves bound together by such wide-ranging variables as language, religious and related convictions, mental and physical habits, rituals and traditions, and biological or geographical ties. The New Rhetoric draws attention to the sociopolitical contexts and interpersonal dynamics of specific messengers and audiences. From this perspective, delineating the extratextual contexts and audiences of a text (e.g., historical circumstances, social phenomena, cultures and customs) is not only helpful, but crucial for understanding the rhetoric of any given community.

The variability of audience reception reminds us that an author can seek to influence using the rhetoric of a text, but persuasion is never guaranteed; persuasive efforts can—and regularly do—exceed or elude the rhetor's control. To adapt Bitzer's formulation, rhetoric's power as a mode of *altering* reality depends on the vagaries of a given audience's responses to it. Reader-response critic Wolfgang Iser describes this in terms of every text's "potential multiplicity of connections," none of which will be absolutely or necessarily realized in the act of interpretation (Iser 1974: 278). Rhetoric, in other words, is risky business.

Of course, these discussions represent but one period in the unending scholarly conversation about rhetoric; the stage had been set for this phase of rhetorical studies in the nineteenth century with figures like Friedrich Nietzsche, who had already begun expanding conceptions of rhetoric's scope and status. Burke's description of rhetoric (cited above) recalls Nietzsche's notes from a lecture course he taught in 1872–73, nearly one hundred years before Burke:

> *There is obviously no unrhetorical "naturalness" of language to which one could appeal; language itself is the result of purely rhetorical arts.* The power to discover and to make operative that which works and impresses, with respect to each thing, a power which Aristotle calls rhetoric, is, at the same time, *the essence of language.*
>
> NIETZSCHE 1989: 21

As a devoted philologist, Nietzsche's reflections on rhetoric grew out of his conceptions about language more generally. His ideas laid the groundwork for linguists like de Saussure and Pierce. These insights, generated in fields and time periods adjacent to modern rhetorical studies, contributed to the twentieth century's expanded notions of rhetoric as a fundamentally hermeneutical, or meaning-making, enterprise.

To sum up this section, the move from classical to modern conceptions of rhetoric is typified by a number of shifts: with the rise of New Rhetoric and modern critical discourse, scholarly attention moved from a dominant focus on the particularities of oral argumentation ("micro-rhetoric") to include conceptions of all language as a constructive form of culture-making ("macro-rhetoric"); from an emphasis on the rhetor's intentions to the varying receptions of interpreting audiences; from fixed notions of categories, or species, of speech to fluid views of communication, texts, and genres.

In addition to these demonstrable shifts, certain issues repeatedly resurface as contested questions in rhetorical studies. One question to which rhetorical theorists return in various iterations is this: To what extent does rhetoric function according to transhistorical, universally-applicable laws, and to what extent is it contingent on the variables of specific communities, time periods, and geographic locations?

1.2.2   The Study of Rhetoric: Recurring Questions

1.2.2.1   *Is Rhetoric General or Contingent?*

Some scholars distinguish between the singular "rhetoric" (i.e., the classical, technical discipline) and the plural "rhetorics" (i.e., specialized or localized ways of thinking and speaking). Although this attempt at terminological precision can be heuristically useful, ambiguities remain—ambiguities that bespeak ongoing contestations over the essence of rhetoric.

On the one hand, the study of "rhetoric" (singular) is *specific* insofar as it concerns a circumscribed set of technical tools and practices from the ancient world. Gérard Genette called this restricted construct a "rhetoric restrained" (Genette 1982). Yet, this conception of rhetoric is simultaneously *general* insofar as it treats those ancient ideas and practices as applicable and persuasive to all humans, regardless of context. The study of *rhetorics* (plural), on the other hand, is a more *generalized* conception of rhetoric insofar as it considers every human to be "essentially a rhetorical animal" (Booth 1974: 134). At the same time, this concept of rhetoric insists that *specific* contexts play a constitutive role in rhetorical meaning-making, and that rhetorical strategies are not equally effective in every time and place. In a sense, then, the latter perspective generalizes specificity.

These conceptions of rhetoric get employed in contemporary textual analysis in two distinct ways. The first, an historical-positivist approach, reads texts in light of the classical Hellenistic guidelines, and assumes that the standard rhetorical canons of invention, arrangement, style, memory, and delivery are stable, timeless, and universally applicable. The second approach considers all textual communication to be rhetorical and contextually-bound, such that textual interpretation requires identifying the variables that make particular people, times, and places unique. Kathleen Welch dubs the former approach the "Heritage School" of interpretation, and the latter, the "Dialectical School" of interpretation (Welch 1990: 3).

The Heritage School is marked by a strong impulse that has long run through rhetorical studies: namely, the desire to legitimate rhetorical analysis by grounding it in objective scientific principles. In the nineteenth century, for example, David Hill wrote *The Science of Rhetoric* (not to be confused with the rhetoric of science; see, e.g., Harris 2013), in which he argues that, like gravity, rhetoric works according to observable, predictable laws. A century later, biblical scholar Roland Meynet echoed the sentiment with his claim that rhetorical analysis provides "*genuine scientific criteria* to delimit the literary units" of a text (Meynet 1998: 316; emphasis added). The Heritage School, accordingly, treats classical rhetoric as an objective, recoverable set of standards by which the critic can judge any text and, ultimately, come to determine its true meaning (Welch 1990: 9). This perspective can be seen in the work of classicist George Kennedy, a leading representative of the Heritage School. For Kennedy, rhetoric is "a universal phenomenon which is conditioned by basic workings of the human mind and heart and by the nature of all human society"; consequently, Kennedy avers, when analyzing literature of *any* place or time period, "we have little choice but to employ the concepts and terms of the Greeks" (Kennedy 1984: 10–11; e.g. Cook 2015).

A potential pitfall of the Heritage approach to textual analysis, however, is that it can easily flatten "ancient rhetoric" into one apparently coherent and consistent system. The ancient evidence overwhelmingly demonstrates the opposite. For one thing, a closer look at actual ancient rhetorical practices and theorizing about rhetoric reveals much more flexible conceptions of rhetoric than the extant technical treatises and handbooks imply. The ancient descriptions of rhetoric found in the progymnasmata are *meant* to systematize and categorize rhetoric; that is their generic purpose. The realities behind these discussions are far messier and more complex. For example, I mentioned above that the handbooks associate certain rhetorical modes with specific locations. And yet, Plato has Socrates ask:

> Must not the art of rhetoric, taken as a whole, be a kind of influencing of the mind by means of words, *not only* in courts of law and other public gatherings, but in private places also? And must it not be the same art that is concerned with great issues and small, its right employment commanding no more respect when dealing with important matters than with unimportant?
>
> *Phaedrus*, 261a–261b; emphasis added

Aristotle, too, assumes that rhetoric is found everywhere, "in reference to any subject whatsoever" (*Rhet.* 1.2.1). And while classical rhetoric provided guidance for the composition of persuasive oratory (i.e., *pre*scription), it also functioned as a rubric by which to analyze the rhetorical effectiveness of existing speeches and other texts (i.e., *de*scription). Divergences between prescriptions and actual practice demonstrate that even in antiquity, rhetoric's definition, its uses, and its value were all fluid and contested (on this point in ancient pedagogical literature, see, e.g., Morgan 1998: 194).

Ancient literature also depicts conflicts about the nature and practice of rhetoric. Porphyry and Iamblichus disagree, Aristotle refutes and revises Plato, Gorgias ridicules Prodicus, Quintilian criticizes Aristotle, and so on. Ekaterina Haskins, for example, has argued that Isocrates and Aristotle advanced "two divergent *literate* logics and two dissimilar visions of discourse, though both rely on oral culture's mythopoetic elements" (Haskins 2004: 30; emphasis original). Disagreements between the two Greek rhetoricians Apollodorus of Pergamon (who taught Augustus) and his younger contemporary Theodorus of Gadara were well-known.[10]

The Dialectical School of rhetorical interpretation recognizes that humans share certain universal experiences (Burke 1931: 149; Booth 1974: 134), but it is also informed by the undeniable fact that specific rhetorical forms and features are persuasive in some contexts and not others. Regarding the question of rhetoric's universality or contingency, many contemporary scholars of rhetoric influenced by the New Rhetoric would say that rhetoric operates according to and/or reflects certain universally-applicable principles, but its meanings and effectiveness change depending on the specific rhetorical situations in which it is employed and interpreted. For example, one general universal principle is that humans are social beings. This is applicable across time, space, and culture. Consequently, human influence flows not just from an individual rhetor to his listener, but also in and through social connections, through the communities in which we live and grow and have our being. At the same time, sociality's role—viz., *how* a given community works to influence, and, conversely, how human influence shapes communities—differs depending on multiple contextual and personal variables.

This brings us to another much-discussed question at the heart of rhetorical studies: If rhetoric's effectiveness is not governed by an individual rhetor's intentions, how should we understand the relationship between rhetoric, the rhetor's intentions, and truth?

1.2.2.2   *How Do Intentionality and Truth Relate to Rhetoric?*

In the introduction, I noted that rhetoric is commonly considered "empty" talk, devoid of substance. Often, when people call others' words "rhetoric,"

---

10   Although Laurent Pernot has helpfully shown that depictions of "Apollodorians" and "Theodorians" as rival sects are exaggerated (Pernot 2005: 159).

they mean to say those words are false. But conceiving of rhetoric solely in terms of truth or falsehood is committing a category error. Rhetorical claims are neither synonymous with nor antonymous with truth claims; they are simply different kinds of claims altogether. Rhetoric is successful if it produces the desired effects, regardless of whether or not those claims are true.

Put differently: Persuasion and its effects are distinct from veracity. Michel Foucault advanced this point in critical theory, describing his own work as an effort "to define the regime of power-knowledge-pleasure that sustains the discourse," *not* "to determine whether these discursive productions and these effects of power lead one to formulate the truth" (Foucault 1978: 11–12). The distinction between rhetoric and truth was assumed in classical rhetorical education. Students were required to practice *disputatio in utramque partem*, or arguing for and against both sides of an issue. Following Aristotle, Cicero tells students to learn "the fluent style of the rhetorician, so that they might be able to uphold either side of the question" (*De Or.* XIV 46); elsewhere, he declares, "We must argue every question on both sides, and bring out on every topic whatever points can be deemed plausible" (*De Or.* I 34). Passages like these make it easy to see how rhetoric can be equated with manipulation. It does sound like Cicero is advocating deceit, or as Americans might say today, "talking out of both sides of one's mouth." However, Cicero's goal is to prepare his students for oratorical debate. In that context, Cicero recognized, rhetoric is about advocating a specific position, which is *distinct from* truth. Focused on effective persuasive strategies in such a setting, Cicero teaches that the successful *rhētor* will anticipate his counterpart's arguments and devise potential responses ahead of time. To warn, as Cicero does, that "a narrative does not guarantee its truth" (Cicero, *De Inv.* I 27) is not to say that a *rhētor*'s narrative is necessarily *un*true; it is to recognize that the truth or falsehood of rhetoric is a separate issue altogether.

Take a modern example. Imagine an attorney who successfully convinces a jury that her client is innocent of murder. She wins her case. She is, in this instance, a successful *rhētor* because the jury found her arguments persuasive; her rhetoric is effective *whether or not* her client actually committed the crime. Conversely, if she had failed to convince the jury to acquit her client, her rhetoric would be unsuccessful, *no matter who* actually murdered the victim. Indeed, this is not just a modern example. Plato recognized this possibility, as well. In fact, this is one reason Plato complained about rhetoric: a skillful lawyer can argue either side of a case successfully, and create actual real-world effects, regardless of whether the final verdict is true or just (*Theatetus* 201a). A person's rhetoric tells us nothing directly about the accuracy or inaccuracy of her or his assertions.

The corollary to this is that rhetoric can be persuasive or not, and thus successful or not, independent of the *rhētor*'s intentions, motivations, or character. We should not automatically impute motives—good or bad—to the *rhētor* based on the words used *or* their effects. A lawyer can convince a jury to acquit a murderer, whether she *intends* to mislead or not. Perhaps her client did murder someone, but she genuinely believes him when he insists that he is innocent; when fighting for an acquittal, then, the attorney believes she is telling the truth, but her claims are factually false. Meanwhile, down the hall in another courtroom, another lawyer could be defending a murderer using the exact same rhetorical strategies, knowing full well that her client is guilty; in the latter case, the lawyer knowingly seeks to persuade the jury of a falsehood, because her job is to win her case. In and of itself, the legal rhetoric employed in the courtroom is not indicative of the lawyer's motivations, intentions, or character.

None of this is to say that truth does not matter at all, or that a *rhētor*'s intentions are inconsequential in matters of persuasion. Both have bearing on the conclusions one draws about a message. This is why Aristotle lists *ēthos*, or "character," as one of the three forms of persuasion: In order to be persuasive, Aristotle advises, a speaker must present himself as credible and trustworthy. Textual interpretation can be particularly tricky in this regard. An author who writes in an ironic or sarcastic tone, for example, *intends* to undercut or overturn the apparent, plain-sense meaning of his own words, but this can be difficult to discern without the "wink and a nudge" of visual and auditory cues, which signal (perhaps playful) insincerity. These interpretive intricacies stand as a crucial caution against rushing to conclusions about truth or falsehood, or about authorial intentions and motivations, based solely on the rhetoric that is employed.

1.2.3   The Study of Rhetoric: Building on and Moving beyond the
          New Rhetoric

Initially, the New Rhetoric's focal point was *verbal* persuasion. In a landmark article from 1953, Donald Bryant *excludes* from rhetoric non-linguistic symbols like "pictures, colors, designs ... fog horns and fire alarms ... traffic lights ... elephants, donkeys, lions ... bottles of whiskey [and] packs of cigarettes"; objects like gold and guns are the province of "commerce or coercion," *not* rhetoric (Bryant 1953: 405). Thus, Bryant asserts, rhetoric properly understood is limited to "the rationale of informative and suasory discourse" (Bryant 1953: 405). This conception of rhetoric's scope remained influential throughout the latter half of the twentieth century.

The New Rhetoric always contained the seeds of its own transformation. The conceptual shifts that it engendered, combined with other theoretical

advancements, such as the rise of cultural and gender studies and poststruc-
turalist theories of language, prompted critical turns toward two other sites
of rhetorical theory and practice in the late twentieth and early twenty-first
centuries: one, I describe as *Multimodal Rhetoric*, and the other, *Metacritical
Rhetoric*.

1.2.3.1   *Multimodal Rhetoric*

Multimodal rhetoric expands beyond verbal rhetoric to consider persuasion
and influence of all kinds. Especially influenced by critical theory's "material
turn," scholars of rhetoric have increasingly recognized that not only words,
but visual images, nonverbal sounds, silences, gestures, embodied movements,
and nondiscursive materialities all send messages. Multimodalism challenges
rhetoric's "empire of the word" (Irigaray 1991: 109), insisting that language is not
the only locus of human communication. A connected conviction is that different modes of communication persuade differently (Burton 1999: 457). If, as
Marshall MacLuhan famously put it, "the medium is the message," then a shift
from one communicative medium to another necessarily changes the message
communicated (MacLuhan 1967: 25). Seeking to increase our understanding of
multimodal forms of communication, these rhetorical theorists now explore
the persuasive potential of all kinds of "texts," including material artwork and
artifacts (e.g., visual rhetoric), place, space, and geography (e.g., spatial rhetoric), the multisensory experiences evoked by and instantiated in the body and
related cognitive processes (e.g., sensory rhetoric, neurorhetoric), new forms
of communication such as hypertexts, blogs, social media platforms (e.g., digi-
tal rhetoric, computational rhetoric), and more.

1.2.3.2   *Metacritical Rhetoric*

A second development for which the New Rhetoric paved the way is *Metacritical
Rhetoric*. The crucial conviction animating metacritical rhetoric is that scholarship about rhetoric also seeks to persuade. Patricia Tull puts it well:

> [R]hetorical criticism (or for that matter any exegetical method) is not
> simply a kind of criticism; it is also a kind of rhetoric. That is to say, it is
> essential to take seriously the rhetorical, persuasive, value-laden nature
> of all discourse. The very practice we are analyzing, we are also ourselves
> exercising, since any stance that an interpreter takes concerning the text
> is by nature a rhetorical stance.
>
> TULL 1999: 163

Metacritical Rhetoric thus expands beyond the rhetoric of specific objects/texts
to consider the rhetorical strategies that scholars employ when discussing

those objects/texts. This mode of rhetorical inquiry turns the critical camera around, submitting scholarly arguments to rhetorical analysis (Zulick 2009: 130–31). The concern here generally remains the persuasive potential of *verbal* communication, because words remain the dominant mode of scholarly communication; it is the text to be evaluated that changes.

If rhetoric about rhetoric is itself rhetorical, then consequently, we should not take rhetoric about rhetoric at face value. This has been true for as long as people have been making claims about the nature of rhetoric. Going back to a previous example: Plato asserted that Sophists intend to mislead. This claim, however, is itself misleading. The Sophists' writings demonstrate that they were not disingenuous or coercive; they simply held a more contextualized view of truth than Plato's singular notion of ideal forms. They emphasized that there are always multiple perspectives from which to analyze an issue. Because their view of truth was more relativistic than Plato's, they advocated a kind of flexible situational ethics with which Plato disagreed. Protagoras's well-known dictum, for instance, declares that "*man* is the measure of all things," *not* an ideal universal truth or objective reality as Plato would have it (Frag. 1, emphasis added). Rather than taking claims about rhetoric as reflective of an unmediated reality "behind" the text, we ought to consider how those claims are rhetorically productive of difference, and function as tools being employed within a given argument.

Consider the scenario, found often in ancient literature, in which a skilled *rhētor* denies having any rhetorical prowess. In the New Testament, for instance, the apostle Paul writes to the believers in Corinth:

> When I came to you, brothers and sisters, I did not come proclaiming the mystery of God to you in lofty words or wisdom. For I decided to know nothing among you except Jesus Christ, and him crucified. And I came to you in weakness and in fear and in much trembling. My speech and my proclamation were not with plausible words of wisdom, but with a demonstration of the Spirit and of power, so that your faith might rest not on human wisdom but on the power of God.
>
> 1 Cor. 2:1–5

Later, in another letter, Paul reiterates: "Even if I am untrained in speaking, I am not so in knowledge; in every way we have made this plain to you in all things" (2 Cor. 11:6). The author of 2 Peter makes a similar claim when he insists, "It was not on tales artfully spun that we relied when we told you of the power of our Lord Jesus Christ and his coming" (2 Pet. 1:16). The fact that the writers make such assertions *as they demonstrate their rhetorical skill* underscores how even disavowed eloquence can be rhetorically motivated.

The disparagement of rhetoric was a longstanding rhetorical trope in antiquity (see, e.g., Hesk 1999). Note, however, that this will only be an effective form of persuasion if an audience suspects that learned eloquence reflects false claims and/or false motives. A literarily sophisticated text will only be perceived as disingenuous sophistry if an audience perceives eloquence as artificial. Burke's notion of *consubstantiality* speaks to this: If rhetoric is to be successful, a persuader must establish a sense of oneness, or identification, with those whom she seeks to persuade (Burke 1953: 21). Proclaiming that one lacks rhetorical skill would only be a compelling rhetorical move for those listeners who identify with the speaker's implication that a *lack* of rhetorical skill signals honesty and reliability.

Conversely, positive evaluations of rhetoric can be just as rhetorically motivated as denigrations of rhetoric. When Isocrates declares that "the most intelligent people use [rhetoric] most of all" (*Nicocles* 6–7), he clearly seeks to situate himself among that number. He also assumes that doing so will be convincing to his audience. Evaluations of rhetoric like Plato's, Paul's, and Isocrates's are not objective observations; they are designed to persuade their audiences of their opinions. Put simply, the heterogeneous assessments of rhetoric found throughout ancient and modern discourse are not neutral; they themselves constitute efforts to influence.

I want to pause for a moment and address an unfortunate tendency in both biblical studies and rhetorical studies proper: Metacritical rhetoric is often distinguished from other forms of rhetoric using the label "ideological." We see this, for example, in Margaret Zulick's entry in *The SAGE Handbook of Rhetorical Studies*—which, it is worth underscoring, is *not* a biblical studies-focused volume. Zulick identifies three separate styles of rhetorical analysis in New Testament scholarship:

1) the *antiquarian* style that applies the classical rhetorical models of Hellenistic rhetoric to the New Testament (i.e., Welch's "Heritage School" of interpretation);

2) the *interactionist* style that incorporates sociopolitical motives when reading New Testament texts (think here of Welch's "Dialectical School");

3) and the *ideological* style that critiques the metadiscourse of New Testament scholarship (Zulick 2009: 130–31).

I submit that Zulick's third category ought to be called *metacritical rhetoric*. The label "ideological" is a misleading misnomer. There are many ways to define "ideology," of course. Eagleton offers a usefully broad definition, drawing on Althusser: "Ideology is ... a particular organization of signifying practices which goes to constitute human beings as social subjects, and which produces the lived relations by which such subjects are connected to the dominant relations of production in society" (Eagleton 1991: 18). Certainly, metacritical rhetoric is ideological in this sense, but so are many other approaches to textual analysis, including the antiquarian and interactional styles that Zulick names separately. What distinguishes metacritical rhetoric is not its style, its perspective on, nor its approach to rhetoric, but its object of study: Metacritical rhetoric turns its gaze to metadiscourse, that is, critical scholarly discourse about rhetoric, which is itself rhetorical.

Naturally, there are wide-ranging and significant consequences when we subject our own work to the same rigorous critique as the texts we aim to interpret. For one thing, rhetorical analysis pushes us to think carefully about how our own rhetoric will impact various audiences differently. Here is a clear example from biblical studies: In a seminal treatment of Paul's rhetoric, *The Corinthian Women Prophets*, Antoinette Clark Wire declares that Paul's "soft spirit" allows him to throw a "blanket of propriety" over his "attempted rape of the women's divine gifts" (Wire 1990: 156). Wire's use of the loaded word "rape" to describe Paul's rhetoric will be jarring, even offensive, to many readers, especially those who are accustomed to imagining Paul the Apostle as a divine stenographer whose self-legitimizing claims ought to stand unquestioned (on moving "beyond the heroic Paul," see Johnson-DeBaufre and Nasrallah 2011). At the same time, the offense itself may be part of Wire's rhetorical strategy, as she provokes her readers to face the grave consequences of Paul's rhetoric subordinating women to men.

Metacritical rhetoric seeks to understand the impact not only of what we claim as scholars, but of *how* we argue for those claims, as well. Explicitly acknowledging that our scholarly discourses are rhetorically crafted, for instance, allows for the fact that they could have been composed otherwise. This commends intellectual humility. No argument should be considered the only or final word on a topic. As Fisher observes, "Adherents of the new rhetoric will hold that ... *no one commands an indisputable position*" (1986: 88). Even scholarly proposals that gain many adherents ought to be regarded as provisional, insofar as they are always perspectival and limited.

Before we turn to the many ways that biblical scholars have appropriated scholarship on rhetoric, I want to highlight several overarching implications of the above developments for the field of biblical scholarship as a whole.

1.2.4 The Study of Rhetoric: General Implications of Modern Rhetorical Studies for Biblical Scholarship

First, modern approaches to rhetoric call for careful attention to the universalities and particularities of biblical rhetoric. On the one hand, all texts are rhetorical; on the other hand, all texts are not rhetorical in the same ways or to the same degrees. In Newsom's terms, "While there can be varying degrees of rhetoric in different acts of communication, all have rhetorical dimensions that can be analyzed" (Newsom 2014: 213). Biblical texts were written by authors from various temporal, geographic, and cultural contexts, for different purposes. We should not assume that rhetoric works the same way in every biblical text. For a number of complicated reasons, including different languages and shifting cultural norms, the Jewish authors of Hebrew Bible texts did not all see the world in the same ways as each other, let alone in the same ways as the Hellenized authors of the Greek New Testament texts. Though there are discernible consistencies in outlook and argumentation across biblical texts, there are also clear differences that we should not elide when seeking to understand their rhetoric.

The second implication of modern rhetorical studies for biblical interpreters is that if we want to understand the rhetoric of each biblical text, we must do the work of historical contextualization, both in terms of situating texts vis-à-vis the contexts in which they arose and in terms of locating the development of biblical canonization and reception chronologically. Rhetoric's emphasis on contextualization reminds us that it is anachronistic and misleading to approach biblical texts as though they made up an established canon of authoritative Scripture any time before the fourth century CE (and even then, the status of certain books continued to be contested). Contrary to the desires of many who wish to honor the Bible as holy Scripture, the assumption that a biblical text has *always* been authoritative actually domesticates it, divesting it of its rhetorical power. Reading in such a way effaces centuries of intense rhetorical combat over canon formation, meaning, truth, and many other related topics. Biblical texts should be read as participants in debates that were already ongoing at the time of their composition, and that continued on after their completion.

Third, the rise of both multimodal and metacritical approaches to rhetorical analysis attests that the boundaries of rhetorical study are constantly shifting. This is a strength, not a weakness. The study of rhetoric is useful for biblical scholarship because the various subdisciplines in biblical studies frame interpretive issues differently, and rhetorical theories clarify how these framings both *enable and constrain* the interpretive possibilities available to us. One of the dangers in our proclivity to stay comfortably within our own habitual intellectual framing is that we can subordinate or ignore the contributions of other orientations, thereby unnecessarily limiting not only our own interpretive insights, but also our own chances for rhetorical success (Booth 2004: 171–72). If we embrace rhetoric's commitment to metacritical analysis, as well as its rigorous interdisciplinarity, we can expand our interpretive horizons without sacrificing critical precision.

Relatedly, metacritical rhetorical analysis makes transparent the fact that the state of contemporary biblical scholarship itself is not objectively self-evident, but the result of particular historical processes. All scholarship is situated, even when it purports to be objective. This is why Burke can refer to the "necessarily suasive nature of even the most unemotional scientific nomenclatures" (Burke 1969: 45). The questions we ask of texts, and the answers we find in them, are determined by the particularities that have shaped us as modern readers. Obviously, the texts we interpret antedate the historical processes that led to our contemporary moment. Consequently, "in every moment of reading, we risk allowing our own perspectives fatally to distort the testimony left behind by others very different from us" (Sharp 2015: 10). Rhetorical studies pushes us to ask a difficult but crucial question: When and how do our modern approaches and assumptions illuminate, and when and how do they obfuscate or distort, the rhetoric of the biblical texts?

Modern rhetorical scholars' attunement to the complicated interstices of intention, tone, content, and impact attests to the need for rhetorical analysis of all texts, but *especially* of Scriptural texts, to which so many turn for guidance in the real world. Rhetorical analysis of biblical literature should be seen *not* as threatening, but as indispensable for those who consider the Bible to be holy Scripture. Those who read the Bible as divinely-inspired Truth will understandably find the concept of rhetorical biblical analysis unpalatable, *if* they take rhetoric to be synonymous with falsehood. But as we have just seen, rhetoric is related to, but distinct from, truth, and related to, but distinct from, authorial intention. To say that the biblical writers seek to persuade says nothing at all about the legitimacy of their truth claims, nor is it necessarily incompatible with the view that biblical texts were divinely inspired. Todd Penner and Davina Lopez are right to insist that rhetorical analysis "is not a matter of accepting the verity of the argumentation itself. It is a matter of seeking to understand the argumentation" (Penner and Lopez 2012: 38). We ought to seek to understand the argumentation—or, to put it in Aristotelian terms, to "discover the possible means of persuasion" (*Rhet.* 1.2.1)—because those means of persuasion shape the kinds of influence that biblical texts wield in the world.

Acknowledging that claims about biblical meaning are themselves rhetorical opens up the space for robust and transparent debate over interpretive criteria and textual meaning-making. Conversely, shutting down the possibility of such conversation is ethically dubious. It makes the interpreter's voice the unquestioned and unquestionable authority. Ironically, ceding authority to the interpreter undermines beliefs that are cherished by many Christians, such as the Protestant concept of *Sola Scriptura*, or the doctrines of inspiration and infallibility. The failure to consider an interpreter's proclamations as rhetorical—whether that interpreter is a scholar, critic, priest, or preacher— puts the locus of power in the interpreter, *not* in the text, as the one to reveal the purported will of God.

Part 2 turns to the many ways that rhetorical scholarship has entered the academic terrain of biblical studies. Getting a full sense for the interactions between these disparate disciplines would require much more space than I have here. Still, just as most languages are spoken in multiple places and in different dialects around the globe, rhetorical study is practiced differently in various locations on the broader map of biblical scholarship, and it can be helpful to know where and by whom that language tends to be used. The various trends in rhetorical analyses of the biblical texts are like local dialects—related but distinct ways of speaking the language of rhetorical studies in different corners of biblical studies. Accepting Bizzell and Herzberg's invitation "to attempt to understand how each [definition of rhetoric] arose and how each still inhabits and shapes the field" (2001: 1), the next section considers how these rhetorical idiolects continue to "inhabit" and "shape" the fields of Hebrew Bible and New Testament scholarship, respectively.

2   Approaches to Biblical Rhetoric

2.1   *Rhetoric in/and Biblical Studies*

Many retrospectives point to Hebrew Bible scholar James Muilenburg's famous 1968 SBL presidential address, "Form Criticism and Beyond," as the point at which rhetorical criticism began to flourish as a definable discourse in biblical scholarship (1969; see also Muilenburg 1953). In his address, notably delivered the same year that the English translation of Perelman and Olbrechts-Tyteca's *The New Rhetoric* appeared, Muilenburg called biblical scholars to move beyond the then-dominant method of form criticism (*Formgeschicht*) toward greater recognition that form and content are irreducibly interrelated in the communicative process (1969: 8). Though Muilenburg valued the form critics' contributions to biblical studies, he insisted that their focus on similarities across texts of a given genre (*Gattung*) led to generalizations and thereby effaced what is "unique and unrepeatable" about each communicative formulation (1969: 5). Muilenburg labeled his enterprise "rhetoric," and his approach "rhetorical criticism" (1969: 8).

Importantly, Muilenburg's emphasis on literary figures like parallelism, asyndeton, and strophic form reflects more than an interest in textual aesthetics or style. His SBL address challenged simplistic approaches that either assumed too much regarding authorship and reception, or failed to take into adequate account the complexities of ancient composition practices and manuscript transmission; even determining what text is in view can prove difficult when it comes to some literature in the Hebrew Bible.

Muilenburg recognized that he was not the first to draw attention to the rhetoric of biblical texts. In his address, he honors his scholarly forebears' interests in rhetoric, which he describes as "style":

> It would be an error, therefore, to regard the modern school in isolation from the history of OT scholarship because from the time of Jerome and before and continuing on with the rabbis and until modern times there have been those who have occupied themselves with matters of style.
>
> MUILENBURG 1969: 8

A decade before Muilenburg, in fact, another SBL president, New Testament scholar Amos Wilder, delivered a presidential address titled, "Scholars, Theologians, and Ancient Rhetoric," in which he proclaimed that biblical scholarship was "at a point where a new cross-fertilization can be helpful from the side of wider humanistic and rhetorical study" (1956: 3; see also Wilder 1971).

Today, rhetorical interpretations of biblical literature have mushroomed far beyond what Wilder or Muilenburg imagined, and publications with "rhetoric" in their title continue to increase in both number and kind. In addition, rhetorical approaches have developed in distinct ways in the subfields of Hebrew Bible scholarship and New Testament scholarship; we turn first to the former.

2.2 *Rhetoric in/and Hebrew Bible Scholarship*

Most twentieth-century discussions of rhetoric in the Hebrew Bible centered on two features of micro-rhetoric that are especially prominent in biblical literature: parallelism and repetition. There are thousands of examples of both. One clear instance of parallelism is the symmetrically-constructed lines of Psalm 103:10:

> Not according to our sins did he deal with us;
> And not according to our transgressions did he requite us.

In this case, the *syntax* between the lines is parallel, but there are many other kinds of parallelism, as well. A *chiasm*, for instance, is a series of inverted parallels. You can envision the structure this way: If A is one idea, and B is another, a chiasm reads:

A
  B
  B′
A′

Often, a chiasm inserts a new idea in the middle for emphasis:

A
  B
    C
  B′
A′

Some biblical passages constitute elaborate, multi-layered chiasms. Consider Isa. 1:21–26:

A 21 How the faithful city
    has become a whore!
  B She that was full of justice,
    righteousness lodged in her—
    but now murderers!
    C 22 Your silver has become dross,
      your wine is mixed with water.
      D 23 Your princes are rebels
        and companions of thieves.
        Everyone loves a bribe
        and runs after gifts.
        They do not defend the orphan,
        and the widow's cause does not come before them.
      D′ 24 Therefore says the Sovereign, the Lord of hosts, the Mighty
        One of Israel:
        Ah, I will pour out my wrath on my enemies,
        and avenge myself on my foes!
    C′ 25 I will turn my hand against you;
      I will smelt away your dross as with lye
      and remove all your alloy.

B′ 26 And I will restore your judges as at the first,
and your counselors as at the beginning.
A′ Afterward you shall be called the city of righteousness,
the faithful city.

Repetition often appears in parallel structures like those above, but it also appears when writers repeat a single word (e.g., "know" in Gen. 3:5), list synonyms (e.g., "all birds, all winged things" in Gen. 7:14), or include entire passages more than once (e.g., the ten commandments in Exod. 20 and Deut. 5). Often, when the same word reappears in Hebrew, English translators substitute synonyms because they assume that repetition is a mark of inferior or formulaic writing, but as Robert Alter and others have shown, it is simply a "misconception" that Hebrew poets composed in "automatic and mechanical" ways (Alter 1985: 13). Repetition and reiteration in the Hebrew Bible should not be regarded as meaningless redundancy (Sternberg 1985: 364–440; Thompson 2018). Even deviations from expected patterns of repetition can have a persuasive function (Freedman 1986). Whether for emphasis, as a mnemonic aid, to clarify or exploit ambiguities, or as a way of "setting in motion a delicate dialectic interplay of meanings," repetitions are used in Hebrew texts to great rhetorical effect (Alter 1985: 17).

Historians of the field often credit the eighteenth-century bishop Robert Lowth with the "discovery" of Hebrew parallelism. Lowth delivered a set of lectures in Oxford in which he famously drew attention to parallelism as a prominent feature of Hebrew poetry (Lowth 1753). In point of fact, Christian Schöttgen had published his volume on Hebrew parallelism, *Horae hebraicae et talmudicae*, in 1733, several decades before Lowth's lectures. Importantly, the discussions of Hebrew rhetoric initiated by Schöttgen and Lowth were fundamentally determined by the classical Greco-Roman tradition. Schöttgen even titled a section of his book, "De Exergasia in genere" (Schöttgen 1733: 1249), referring to the rhetorical figure of *exergasia* (when an idea is repeated, but stated differently the second time).[11] As Jacqueline Vayntrub notes from a metacritical perspective, "the 'discovery' of parallelism in biblical poetry was not theoretically neutral" (Vayntrub 2019: 49). Indeed, throughout the eighteenth, nineteenth, and even into the twentieth centuries, scholars discussed Hebrew prosody using the vocabulary of classical Greek and Roman rhetorical conventions. They reflected Kennedy's assumption (cited above) that,

---

11   Quintilian and Aristotle discuss *exergasia* in their rhetorical handbooks (e.g., Quint. *Inst. Or.* 8.5; Arist. *Rhet.* 2.21).

when analyzing literature from *any* time or place, "we have little choice but to employ the concepts and terms of the Greeks" (Kennedy 1984: 11).

But ancient Hebraic rhetoric was established centuries before rhetoric's classical age had even begun. Clearly, the writers of Israel's oldest texts were aware of the practices and processes of rhetoric; the priests and prophets of Israel are portrayed as persuasive speakers, and we can easily identify instances in the Hebrew Bible of rhetorical figures such as those that Aristotle and others later outlined and classified. The more important point is that rhetoric had not been systematized or theorized by the Greeks and Romans yet. The literature of the Hebrew Bible ought to be appreciated for its own distinctive expressive virtues, separate from the standards and rules of the Greeks or the Romans. Scholars who oppose "employ[ing] the concepts and terms of the Greeks" to describe Hebrew literature (e.g., Meynet 1990: 312–13, 1998: 172–77; Pernot 2005: 6) also point out that the many and varied texts of the Hebrew Bible have complicated compositional histories, and that their relation to Hellenism remains an open discussion (Thompson and Wajdenbaum 2014; Grabbe 2001). Such critics rightly warn against the intellectual imperialism that comes so naturally to Western inheritors of the classical Greco-Roman tradition.

In the latter half of the twentieth century, scholars such as James Kugel and Adele Berlin critiqued Lowth's concept of parallelism as too narrow. Recasting parallelism as more than a simple correspondence between adjacent words or lines, both Kugel and Berlin argued that many kinds of parallelism characterize not only Hebrew poetry, but all biblical literature (Kugel 1981; Berlin 1985). Berlin's *The Dynamics of Biblical Parallelism* demonstrates from a modern linguistic perspective how, in order to grasp parallelism's rhetorical effectiveness, one ought to assess the dynamic "interplay of equivalences" at work in its syntactic, morphologic, lexical, and semantic aspects (Berlin 1985: 30). Kugel and Berlin represent a larger shift in twentieth-century biblical scholarship, as scholars increasingly engaged the work of literary structuralists in their efforts to do justice to the unique features of Hebrew Bible literature. More recently, Vayntrub has argued that quests for the "essence" of Hebrew poetry are constrained by modern literary categories into which biblical literature does not fit, and that these efforts ultimately fall short, revealing "the limitations of our aesthetics to account for biblical aesthetics" (2019: 59).

Over the past decade, scholars like F. W. Dobbs-Allsopp have explored the rhetoric of Hebrew poetry from a different direction. Dobbs-Allsopp analyzes the significance of poetic formatting in Hebrew Bible manuscripts. Metascript conventions such as *lineation*, the arrangement of words on a page according to set line lengths (as opposed to running out of available space), not only serve as visual cues to readers, signaling that a text is poetic; they also render certain aural and rhythmic features of the language more or less pronounced (Dobbs-Allsopp 2015: 174). For example, in his discussion of *enjambment*, a sentence or phrase that runs over into the next line (as opposed to end-stopped lines, which convey a completed thought), Dobbs-Allsopp observes that in Lamentations, enjambed and end-stopped lines "play off" of one another, providing a way for the poet "to promote a sense of movement and control the pace" of the text (Dobbs-Allsopp 2015: 137). Projects like Dobbs-Allsopp's cohere well with Muilenburg's conception of rhetorical criticism, the goal of which was to understand "the structural patterns that are employed for the fashioning of a literary unit, whether in poetry or in prose" (1969: 8).

In the ensuing decades after Muilenburg's address, scholars refined his rhetorical approach and brought it to bear on specific biblical books. Two of Muilenburg's students were especially influential: Jack Lundbom and Phyllis Trible. In addition to other works, Lundbom's 1973 dissertation, *Jeremiah: A Study in Ancient Hebrew Rhetoric* (dedicated to Muilenburg and published unrevised in 1997), supports Muilenburg's challenge to move "beyond" form criticism by arguing that "Jeremianic discourse is structured not according to form-critical models but according to canons of ancient Hebrew rhetoric" (Lundbom 1997: xxxv; more recently, see Lundbom's own textbook on rhetorical biblical criticism 2013). Phyllis Trible's *Rhetorical Criticism: Context, Method, and the Book of Jonah* introduces the intellectual backgrounds and foregrounds of Muilenburg's rhetorical program, and then analyzes the book of Jonah to demonstrate how "Yhwh seeks to persuade Jonah, judge and complainant, to make a right decision about past events" (Trible 1994: 224).

Eventually, Hebrew Bible scholars came to regard Muilenburg's approach to rhetoric as too limited. Though Muilenburg himself explicitly rejected the label "stylistics" in his SBL address, this was overwhelmingly the sense in which scholars understood his approach. Note the repeated refrain running through descriptions of his work: Muilenburg's rhetorical criticism is "the study of stylistics of composition in Hebrew prose and poetry" (Dozeman 1992: 713–15), "primarily a literary concern, with emphasis upon stylistics" (Howard 1994: 87), and "an expression of stylistic-formalist awareness rather than a systematic study of early Hebrew rhetoric, the biblical art of persuasion" (Gitay 1993: 136). Tull finds it ironic that "Muilenburg's use of the term 'rhetorical criticism' to refer to stylistic analysis reflected the very reduction that had helped signal rhetoric's eclipse in earlier centuries" (1999: 156). Lundbom, while appreciative of his teacher's contributions, notes that when compared to rhetorical studies elsewhere in the university, Muilenburg's program of rhetorical criticism was "perceived by many as being little more than an exercise in textual description" (Lundbom 1997: xxviii). Nearly twenty years after Muilenburg delivered his address, Wilhelm Wuellner wrote a programmatic article titled "Where Is Rhetorical Criticism Taking Us?" in which he argued that rhetorical criticism was nothing more than "an estheticizing preoccupation with biblical stylistics which has remained for centuries formalized, and functionless, and contextless" (1987: 462).

The New Rhetoric's more expansive treatments of rhetoric are reflected in a number of rhetorical interpretations in Hebrew Bible scholarship after Muilenburg. In the early 1980s, Alter, for instance, published his now-classic treatments of biblical literature, *The Art of Biblical Narrative* (1981) and *The Art of Biblical Poetry* (1985), both of which are keenly sensitive to the formal features of poetry and prose as persuasive communication. In *The Art of Biblical Narrative*, Alter masterfully elucidates "the *range of* intended meanings—theological, psychological, moral, or whatever—of the biblical tale" (Alter 1981: 179; emphasis added), in part by highlighting the rhetorical abilities of specific characters: King David is "a master of rhetoric," God's Adversary in the book of Job is "a master of conscious rhetoric, alongside of whom God seems plainspoken," and Hushai in the story of Absalom's rebellion delivers "a brilliant rhetorical contrivance, abounding in persuasive similes" (Alter 1981: 189, 193). These characters' rhetorical prowess, for Alter, reflects and instantiates the rhetorical power of the texts themselves.

In 1985, the same year that Alter's *The Art of Biblical Poetry* appeared, Meir Sternberg published *The Poetics of Biblical Narrative*. Sternberg, like Alter, treats ideology, rhetoric, and formal features of narrative as "indistinguishable" (1985: 35). His analysis focuses primarily on the narration, or discourse (what he calls the poetics), of Hebrew Bible narratives. Sternberg argues that the rhetorical intentions of the biblical writers so shaped their storytelling that the narrator becomes a "persuader," a "rhetorician" who "seeks not just to affect but to affect with a view to establishing consensus in the face of possible demur and opposition" (1985: 482). The biblical persuader does so, moreover, by drawing on his "rhetorical repertoire" of specific storytelling strategies (1985: 475). For example, Sternberg writes that the biblical narrator strategically employs ambiguity in order to "artfully exploit" the audience's "reluctance or inability to wait until the end for closures that may never come" (1985: 199).

Rhetoric plays a crucial role in more recent readings of biblical narrative, as well. In 2016, Danna Nolan Fewell reflected that transdisciplinary theoretical advancements had produced "a veritable academic industry addressing the relationships between knowledge and narrative," and consequently, "'the art of biblical narrative' (Alter 1981) now makes room for 'the work of biblical narrative,' namely, what biblical stories accomplish cognitively, socially, and ethically, for good and ill, both as literary artifacts of the ancient world and as living literary specimens that continue to shape contemporary cultures and individual identities" (Fewell 2016: 2).

In addition to the rhetoric of narrative discourse, other communicative modes in the Hebrew Bible have been read through a self-consciously rhetorical lens, including prophetic rhetoric (Gitay 1981, 2001); apocalyptic rhetoric (Kaltner 1999; Newsom 2019); and ironic rhetoric (Sharp 2009). Some scholars analyze rhetoric not in terms of stylistic traits or established generic categories, but from a thematic perspective (i.e., macro-rhetoric). Discussing a text's macro-rhetoric can take the form of an argument regarding an author's rhetorical intentions. Amy Kalmanofsky, for instance, argues that the author of Jeremiah crafts a "rhetoric of horror" (especially in the "horror corpus" of Jer. 4:5–6:30; 8:1–22; 13:15–27) in order to persuade the people of Israel to rely on God (Kalmanofsky 2008). Or reading a text's macro-rhetoric can mean tracing the reception history of a particular theme. For example, Jonathan Lamb delineates how eighteenth-century interpreters read the "rhetoric of suffering" in the book of Job in order to contend with conflicting theories about suffering and justice in their own day (Lamb 1995).

Certain contemporary Hebrew Bible scholars focus especially on how texts employ persuasive techniques in service of ancient political, social, or cultural ideologies. In Foucauldian terms, these critics are interested in unmasking the relations of power that "pass[ed] through systems of communication" in antiquity (Foucault 1988: 18). Trible, for instance, has pushed biblical interpreters to engage feminism, which she defines as "a critique of culture in the light of misogyny" (Trible 1994: 7). Famously labeling misogynistic biblical passages "texts of terror," Trible attempts to restore what she sees as the original egalitarian meaning of the Torah (Trible 1994). Following Trible, other feminist scholars have similarly sought to expose the biblical depictions of women as rhetorical constructions. Tammi Schneider, for example, emphasizes the biblical matriarchs' valuable role as guarantors of racial and religious purity—rhetorical reminders, that is, of the dangers of exogamy (Schneider 2008). These treatments of biblical rhetoric, while focused on situating texts within their ancient contexts, draw on and contribute to modern critical discourses such as postcolonial, minority, masculinist, and Queer theories, all of which interrogate rhetorical justifications of oppressive and exclusionary power dynamics.

2.3   *Rhetoric in/and New Testament Scholarship*

As I already mentioned, Amos Wilder's SBL address of 1955 proposed a new focus on rhetoric in biblical studies. Though his address did not initiate a field-wide rhetorical turn, Wilder's own publications consistently explored the rhetoric of the New Testament through existential and theological lenses. In his classic 1964 volume, *Early Christian Rhetoric*, Wilder argues that the Gospels function rhetorically to elicit relational responses between their human audiences and the divine:

> [T]he personal dramatic character of the Gospel itself necessarily involves ... the living encounter of heart and heart, voice and voice ... this has inevitably registered itself in the ongoing story of the Christ and in the style of the New Testament.
>
> WILDER 1971: 54

Drawing on the Bultmannian theological interpretive movement called the "New Hermeneutic," Wilder and others (e.g., Funk 1966) held that biblical rhetoric instantiates a peculiar kind of language event, in and through which one encounters God. Wilder's underlying Christian conviction is that the rhetoric of the New Testament, which he deems "simple," reflects "the way things are and the way things happen" (Wilder 1971: 125).

The most popular form of rhetorical analysis in New Testament scholarship since the mid- to late twentieth century has been the Heritage School of interpretation (Welch's term; see above). These critics seek to identify and classify instances in New Testament texts of rhetorical techniques and compositional conventions found in the ancient progymnasmata and rhetorical handbooks (helpful overviews include Mack 1990: esp. 25–48 and Parsons and Martin 2018). At first, such appeals to classical rhetorical conventions were considered an additional set of tools with which to do historical work. Kennedy, for example, begins his classic introduction, *New Testament Interpretation through Rhetorical Criticism*, by declaring that a rhetorical approach will assist those who are interested in "reading the Bible as it would be read by an early Christian" (Kennedy 1984: 5).

It comes as no surprise that Pauline scholars were among the first to use this form of rhetorical analysis; Paul's epistles had already long been seen as self-conscious attempts to persuade his audiences toward particular convictions and actions. A quintessential example is Hans Dieter Betz's 1979 Hermeneia commentary on Paul's letter to the Galatians. There, Betz proposes that Galatians is an apologetic letter, a type of *forensic rhetoric*.[12] In a review of the volume, David Aune observes:

> The single most innovative feature of this commentary is, I would judge, the author's proposed analysis of the surface structure of Paul's letter to the Galatians in terms of Greco-Roman rhetorical theory.
>
> AUNE 1981: 323–24

---

12   See also Betz 1975, 1985, and 1995.

Some have disputed Betz's conclusions about Galatians, if not his Heritage School approach (e.g., Classen 1991; Tolmie 2005), while others have applied the same approach to different New Testament texts. As an example of the latter, Margaret Mitchell, one of Betz's students, reads the entirety of 1 Corinthians as *deliberative rhetoric*, or "argumentation which urges an audience, either public or private, to pursue a particular course of action in the future" (Mitchell 1991: 24; other influential examples include Stowers 1981, 1994; Jewett 1986; Olbricht and Sumney 2001; Watson 2006).

Though most scholarly publications in this vein focus on New Testament epistolary literature, some critics have brought classical Greco-Roman conventions to bear on New Testament narratives, as well. In Gospel studies, many have drawn attention to Jesus' frequent use of the *chreia*, a highly popular ancient rhetorical form defined as "a recollection of a saying or action or both, with a pointed meaning, usually for the sake of something useful" (Pseudo-Hermogenes, *Prog.* 19; e.g., Mack and Robbins 1989). Some scholars have read the public speeches in the book of Acts as formal classical oratories. Stanley Porter, for instance, categorizes Paul's eight public speeches in this way: Paul uses *deliberative* rhetoric to persuade his audiences to believe the gospel in missionary speeches at Pisidian Antioch (13:16–41), at Lystra (14:15–17), and on the Areopagus in Athens (17:22–31; cf. Brawley, who considers Acts 17:27–28 to be *epideictic* rhetoric; Brawley 1995: 127); Paul employs *forensic* rhetoric to defend his own actions in apologetic speeches before the Jerusalem Jews (22:1–21), the procurator Felix (24:10–21), Herod Agrippa (26:2–23), and the Roman Jewish leaders (28:17–20); and he uses *epideictic* rhetoric to encourage those he leaves behind in a farewell speech before the Miletan elders (notably, his only oration before a Christian audience, 20:18–35; Porter 2013).

The classical Heritage mode of rhetorical criticism makes two assumptions that are contested in current New Testament scholarship. The first concerns the New Testament writers' levels of education: this approach assumes that New Testament writers knew of and intentionally used classical rhetorical conventions. However, we do not know the extent or nature of the earliest Jesus followers' educations. This is a complicated issue. Most of our extant evidence about ancient education comes from the elite strata of society, and is therefore limited to a narrow slice of the population. We do know that we cannot assume a homogenous continuity between modern views on education and the ways that education functioned in the first century CE. Accordingly, in recent decades, classicists have been working to "render the constituent elements of the [ancient] pedagogical scenario open to negotiation" (Too 1998, 2000, 2001; Cribiore 2001; Walker and Benson 2012).

We also know that most people at the time were unable to write and/or read (these were distinct skills, taught and practiced separately), so the very fact that the New Testament writers compose their own prose and cite other texts attests to a relatively high level of education. At the same time, the New Testament texts are written in *koine* (common) Greek, not the more sophisticated classical Greek that typified an elite Greco-Roman education, which leads some scholars to conclude that the writers had not been formally trained. Porter, for instance, concludes that none of the New Testament writers was even aware of classical rhetoric, because "becoming an accomplished rhetorician … took specialized training, which was usually reserved for only a few elite men who had considerable financial means" (Porter 1993: 652). Yet, Kennedy and others argue that rhetorical oratorical principles so pervaded the ancient Mediterranean that "even those without formal education necessarily developed cultural preconceptions about appropriate discourse" (Kennedy 1984: 5).

The New Testament itself rarely refers to rhetoric in a classical sense. Though the texts frequently mention verbal persuasion, such as advocating "bold speech" (*parrēsia*) on behalf of Christ (e.g., Acts 13:46; 14:3; 18:26; 19:8; 1 Thess. 2:2; Eph. 6:20; Phil. 1:14), there is only one mention of rhetoric as *technē*: The book of Acts refers to Tertullus, a "rhetor" (*rhētoros Tertullou*) who helps Ananias bring legal charges against Paul (Acts 24:1). In the end, we know little about how the New Testament writers were educated, or whether they were aware of theoretical rhetorical treatises like Aristotle's *Rhetoric*.

The second contested matter regarding classical rhetorical criticism in New Testament studies is the issue of authorial intent. Practitioners of the classical approach often prioritize authorial intent as determinative of meaning. However, as discussed above, ancient rhetoricians and theorists recognized that a rhetor's intent does not dictate whether his language will be rhetorically successful. To my mind, the New Rhetoric's focus on rhetoricity as a feature of all texts provides a useful way of grappling with the fact that New Testament texts were written to persuade, without resorting to reductive concepts of authorial intent as the only or even the dominant factor in meaning-making (Dinkler 2019). We can consider the persuasive potential of extolling virtues, for instance, without arguing that the author consciously intended to employ the classical category of *epideictic rhetoric*.

The 1980s and 90s gave rise to what Jan Botha called a "reinvention of rhetoric" in biblical studies (Botha 1989; see, e.g., Siegert 1985; Wire 1990). This "reinvention" was not univocal. For some, modern approaches like the New Rhetoric represented a direct and fatal critique of the Heritage approach. J. D. Hester Amador, for instance, using a phrase from Gérard Genette, called classical rhetorical criticism a "rhetoric restrained," arguing that the latter is "overly focused on form and style" and not focused enough on "power and rhetoricity" (Hester Amador 1999: 1). Others, such as Antoinette Clark Wire, sought to maintain the classical categories, but situate them within the New Rhetoric's broader focus on "illuminating how words function to persuade" (Wire 1990: 2):

> The major distinctions in the ancient discipline are retained ... But the study of rhetoric has changed significantly; its scope is both broader and more clearly delimited than before, and there is a concomitant change in the precision of its work.
>
> WIRE 1990: 2

Although Wire does not read through a classical antiquarian lens, her aim in attending to Paul's rhetoric remains historical: She seeks to "reconstruct as accurate a picture as possible of the women prophets in the church of first-century Corinth" (Wire 1990: 1). Treating Paul's rhetoric as "a window into a volatile situation," Wire concludes that 1 Corinthians is Paul's rhetorical argument against a group of women prophets who were challenging his restrictive views about women in leadership (Wire 1990: 3).

While some participants in rhetoric's "reinvention" in New Testament studies drew explicitly from the well of Perelman and Olbrechts-Tyteca's New Rhetoric (e.g., Siegert 1985), others assimilated the shifts in modern rhetoric more implicitly. Vernon Robbins's brand of rhetorical inquiry, known as *sociorhetorical criticism*, is less explicitly tied to the New Rhetoric, even as they share several core premises. Drawing together insights from a range of earlier thinkers, including Wilder on early Christian discourse, Wuellner on hermeneutics, and Burke on humanity's "archetypal drama," Robbins and his colleagues analyze texts as multiple "textures" woven together (inner texture, intertexture, social and cultural texture, and ideological texture; see, e.g., Robbins 1996). They also distinguish between "oral culture," "scribal culture," "rhetorical culture," and "print culture," ultimately identifying the culture of Mediterranean antiquity as "rhetorical"—by which they mean an environment "where oral and written speech interact closely with one another" (Robbins 1991: 148). As a part of this "rhetorical culture," Robbins argues, early Christians employed various "rhetorolectic forms":

> [F]irst century Christians created at least six forms of radicalized worldly rhetoric—apocalyptic, prophetic, miracle, wisdom, precreation, and priestly—and by the fourth century they successfully launched creedal rhetoric.
>
> ROBBINS 2008: 87–88

Robbins's approach has developed into a distinct school of interpretation complete with its own monograph series, the Rhetoric of Religious Antiquity series published by Deo. More recently, sociorhetorical criticism has expanded beyond written texts (and thus, into a form of multimodal rhetoric) to explore what its practitioners call *rhetography*, or how written and visual imageries intersect in the minds of readers (e.g., Jeal 2013; Robbins 2008; deSilva 2008).

The New Rhetoric's emphasis on verbal persuasion appears in a different way in narrative-critical and reader-response approaches to New Testament narratives (e.g., Black 2001). Along the lines of Hebrew Bible scholars such as Alter, Sternberg, and Berlin, New Testament scholars began to recognize that while early Christian narratives had been "endlessly read through, or read around, they [had] all too seldom been read on their own terms" (Anderson and Moore 2008: 10). In Robert Fowler's words, New Testament texts "take aim at the reader" (Fowler 1991: 23). Subsequent attempts to read these stories "on their own terms" led to a newfound focus on how a narrative's formal features function rhetorically to persuade their audiences. Rather than asking, "*What* does the story mean?" these New Testament critics asked, "*How* does the story mean?" (Malbon 2008). The latter question is centrally concerned with the story's rhetoric, even if the term rhetoric itself does not appear (Dinkler 2016; 2020).

Overall, New Testament scholars remain predominantly interested in classical rhetoric, and the resources of modern rhetorical studies remain underutilized (Porter 2017: 650–51).

2.4   *Metacritical Rhetoric in/and Biblical Scholarship*

Already in this volume, I have mentioned two SBL presidential addresses that called for new rhetorically-oriented approaches to biblical literature (Wilder's in 1955, and Muilenburg's in 1968). Twenty years after Muilenburg's address, Elisabeth Schüssler Fiorenza began her presidential address, titled, "The Ethics of Biblical Interpretation: Decentering Biblical Scholarship," with this self-reflexive observation: "It is a commonplace that presidential addresses have primarily rhetorical functions" (Schüssler Fiorenza 1988: 1). Schüssler Fiorenza's own rhetorical goal was to inaugurate a new rhetorical turn in biblical studies. This phase, which she labeled the "rhetorical-ethical" or "rhetorical-emancipatory" paradigm, ought to exhibit "self-understanding of scholarship as communicative praxis" (Schüssler Fiorenza 1988: 4).

Despite Schüssler Fiorenza's tremendous influence in certain corners of biblical studies, her SBL address ultimately did not give rise to a "rhetorical-ethical" turn in the field broadly. A decade later, Schüssler Fiorenza reiterated her call for "practitioners of biblical studies and readers of the Bible to become ethically more sophisticated readers," writing that the rhetorical-emancipatory paradigm:

> ... invites them to problematize both the modernist ethos of biblical studies and their own sociopolitical locations and functions in global structures of domination. At the same time it enables biblical readers to struggle for a more just and radical democratic cosmopolitan articulation of religion in a global context.
>
> SCHÜSSLER FIORENZA 1999: 57

Perhaps Schüssler Fiorenza has not persuaded more biblical scholars to adopt this mode of rhetorical analysis due to the persistent perception that rhetoric itself is biased and skewed and therefore inherently antithetical to the scholarly enterprise.

Some assert that Schüssler Fiorenza's own pointed rhetoric is counterproductive. Robbins charges her with using combative language, characterized by "inner attributes of domination and separation that she claims she would like to move beyond" (Robbins 2002: 51):

> Rather than opening a conversation about how one might negotiate a disagreement about the intertextual construction of a particular context for interpretation, Schüssler Fiorenza closed down a discussion of the issue with oppositional rhetoric ...
>
> ROBBINS 2002: 51

Others defend Schüssler Fiorenza, responding that Robbins mischaracterizes her views (e.g., Fuchs 2003; Marchal 2006: 7). While some adamantly echo Schüssler Fiorenza's critiques of biblical studies as a discipline, at this point, contemplating the intersections of rhetoric, ethics, and interpretation remains a goal shared by select groups of critics, rather than a larger discipline-wide movement. In another sense, though, we could consider the fact that Schüssler Fiorenza's own rhetoric has been the focus of rhetorical battles as a successful instantiation of the very metacritical approach she seeks to advocate.[13]

Though biblical studies has not exactly entered a "rhetorical-ethical" phase, biblical scholars have generally become more attentive to their own interpretive practices. Metacritique appears more frequently in both Hebrew Bible and New Testament scholarship with each passing year. Metacritical rhetorical analysis can "witness to different forms and degrees of oppression in

---

13   See Schüssler Fiorenza 1996 and Robbins's 2002 rejoinder.

patriarchal religious institutions, the academy, and societies" in a number
of ways and with various foci (Anderson 1992: 113). Some critics draw upon
postcolonial theory in order to illuminate the politics involved in translating,
interpreting, and canonizing biblical texts (see Sugirtharajah 2005; Runesson
2007). Others argue that efforts to recuperate or redeem oppressive biblical
texts for contemporary communities are themselves oppressive—or at best,
misguided. Elizabeth Clark, for instance, insists that scholars must not ignore
how models of female submission have always served as rhetorical mecha-
nisms for patriarchal control, and that even biblical texts that portray female
figures positively can subtly serve as "strategies of containment" for women in
patriarchal systems (Clark 2004: 176).

Rhetorical "strategies of containment" continue to shape biblical scholarship today, as do more liberative and transgressive rhetorical strategies. The
fact that this scholarly rhetoricity is not immediately obvious and typically
remains unacknowledged, is why it is so vital for biblical scholars to subject
our own and others' rhetoric to the rigorous, detailed analysis that we seek to
bring to our primary sources.

My goals in Parts 1–2 were to identify major trends in rhetorical studies as
a field, and to introduce the main ways that scholars have approached the
rhetoric of biblical literature. But as teachers of rhetoric have always claimed,
abstract didactic instruction *about* rhetoric can only go so far. True learning
requires examples, modeling, and repeated practice. Part 3 analyzes the rhetoric of the First Epistle of Peter in order to demonstrate the benefits of various
forms of rhetorical interpretation with a specific biblical text.

3   Reading the Rhetorics of First Peter

Some aspects of the *rhetorical situation* that gave rise to the First Epistle of
Peter are clear. Generally dated to the late first or early second century CE, the
letter is addressed to "the elect exiles (*parepidēmois*) of the Dispersion (*diaspora*) in Pontus, Galatia, Cappadocia, Asia, and Bithynia" (1:1).[14] While most
agree that the salutation alludes to the experiences of displaced Israelites
in the Jewish diaspora, scholars part ways regarding the sense in which the
Petrine recipients experienced diaspora. Some read the reference as metaphorically depicting Christians' spiritual sojourn on earth while awaiting their
true heavenly home, while others view this language as referring to Christians'

---

14   Michaels classifies 1 Peter as a "diaspora letter," which was "a well-known means of formal
        communication from Jerusalem to Jewish communities scattered in Babylon, Assyria,
        or Egypt." Michaels 1988: xlvi.

actual socio-legal "outsider" status post-conversion in the Roman Empire (representative of the former are Martin 1990; Chin 1991; Feldmeier 1992; representative of the latter are Williams 2012; Elliott 1981; Elliott 2000: 482).[15] Either way, the *exigence* that the pseudonymous author (hereafter, called Peter) seeks to address, according to the epistle itself, is that the addressees face some form of suffering and persecution because they have chosen to follow Jesus. 1 Peter 4:16 encapsulates the situation: "Yet if any of you suffers as a Christian (*Christianos*),[16] do not consider it a disgrace, but glorify God because you bear this name." The vocabulary of suffering permeates the letter (e.g., *lupeō*, "to feel pain" in 1:6; *lupē* in 2:19; *paschō*, "to suffer" in 2:19, 20, 21, 23; 3:14, 17, 18; 4:1 [twice], 15, 19; 5:10).[17] So prominent is the theme of suffering that Frank Matera calls 1 Peter "the most comprehensive theology of suffering in the New Testament" (2007: 381; cf. Thorsteinsson 2010: 107).[18] Secondary themes such as growing in salvation (2:1–5), proper behavior outside and inside the household (2:13–3:12), and "shepherding" God's flock (5:1–4) are related to this main focus.

3.1   The "Rhetorical Situation" and Historical Backgrounds

Our working definition of rhetoric (cited above) is: "the political effectivity of trope and argument in culture" (Mailloux 1989: xii). In order to understand 1 Peter's political effectivity in its culture(s) of origin, we must situate its tropes and arguments in the historical contexts "behind" the letter. These historical contexts constitute the "rhetorical situation" that informed the epistle's composition. In this sense, rhetorical exigence makes a difference for rhetorical exegesis, and our best attempts at historical reconstruction therefore play an important role in rhetorical analysis.

Efforts to (re)construct the epistle's historical background have focused especially on determining the precise nature of the suffering and persecution to which 1 Peter refers. Though the extent of official imperial persecution

---

15   Elliott posits a chronological development from an actual exile to a metaphorical one in Elliott 2000.

16   Paul Trebilco contends that early on, the term "Christian" was used in a "mocking" or "pejorative" way in "an outsider-facing situation," and that it only later became "insider" language (Trebilco 2004: 554–56).

17   I recognize the problems inherent in the uncritical conflation of "suffering and persecution" and/or "suffering and pain" that one often finds in both common parlance and academic discourse. These are slippery concepts; people can "persecute" or "be persecuted" in various ways, perceptions of what constitutes suffering and/or persecution differ in various communities, and one person's subjective threshold for "pain" might differ from another's.

18   Differences between the first and second halves of the letter vis-à-vis the language of suffering have given rise to various theses about the circumstances of 1 Peter's addressees. On partition theories, see Williams 2012: 340–49.

of Christians throughout the first two centuries CE has long been debated
(on which, see, e.g., Bovon 1978), some believe that 1 Peter was written between
70 and 95 CE, when Roman persecution of Christians was generally sporadic
and localized (e.g., Elliott 2000: 135–38), and others read it in a context of man-
dated Empire-wide persecution (e.g., Achtemeier 1996: 29–33; Williams 2012:
5–15). Historical-critical scholars have sought to identify the exact referent of
the "fiery ordeal" (*purōsei*) in 4:12 (see also 1:6–7),[19] and to explain the nature of
the letter's exile/alien language (1:1, 17; 2:11).[20]

A modern rhetorical approach to 1 Peter inflects historically-oriented questions about suffering and persecution differently. Rhetorical analysis insists
that whatever the *actual* historical realities might have been, the text's references to suffering and persecution are rhetorical insofar as they are being used
to contribute to the epistle's persuasive message(s). We cannot access the real
historical Peter "behind" the text, nor can we access the actual historical circumstances in which he or his recipients lived; we can only access the rhetorical world that (the person whom we call) Peter constructed in and through
the extant epistle. When Peter writes that the Gentiles are "surprised" that his
recipients "no longer join" them "in the same excesses of dissipation" (4:4), and
when he tells his readers not to be "surprised" by the "fiery ordeal taking place"
among them (4:12), whatever concrete realities such references may or may
not refer to, one thing we can say for certain: *This is rhetoric.* Newsom's advice
is helpful: "Just as one distinguishes between the actual author of a text and
the implied author constructed by the text, so one might think in terms of an
implied rhetorical situation called into being by the text" (Newsom 2018: 8).

Authors like Peter are always "busily constructing a rhetorical world, a world
of advice and consent, of persuasion and dissuasion, inculcating certain beliefs
and behaviors" by participating in multiple rhetorical discourses of meaning-
making that are already ongoing in their sociocultural contexts (Witherington
2009: 177). Suffering represents one such discourse. 1 Peter is but one among
many voices discussing suffering; as other contemporaneous evidence demonstrates, wider ancient discourses about suffering were being put to powerful rhetorical use elsewhere, not least by other Christians. In her classic study,
The Suffering Self: Pain and Narrative in the Early Christian Era, Judith Perkins
argues that early Christians' foregrounding of their own suffering provided a

---

19   Reicke asserts that *purōsei* refers to literal martyrdom (1964: 71–72; cf. Borchert 1982:
      451–52).
20   For a nuanced discussion of the "resident alien *topos*" in 1 Peter, see Dunning 2008: 9–13.
      Paul Himes helpfully outlines scholarly views of the displacement terminology in Himes
      2014: 40–73.

unique self-definition for the nascent Christian movement (Perkins 1995: 13). "To be a Christian," declares Perkins, "was to suffer" (1995: 205). Perkins is right, although it is also important not to assume that depictions of suffering in early Christian texts all function similarly (e.g., Talbert 1991: 9; Williams 2012: 15). Early Christian rhetoric about suffering reveals remarkable diversity in terms of 1) the experiences that are labeled suffering (reference); 2) the causes of suffering (reason); and 3) the ideal behavior of Christians who face suffering (response). Increasingly, scholars have nuanced Perkins's observations to account for the fact that not all early Christians agreed about what constitutes suffering, what causes suffering, or how one ought to respond to suffering (e.g., Williams 2012; King 2013).

Momentarily, I shall show how attending to 1 Peter's rhetoric facilitates the task of differentiating its claims about the references to, reasons for, and commended responses to suffering. First, however, I present a brief outline of how modern scholars have approached the rhetoric of 1 Peter thus far.

3.2 *Previous Approaches to Petrine Rhetoric*

Several studies appeared in the late twentieth century that approached 1 Peter in the classical Heritage mode of rhetorical criticism described above. A well-known example is Barth Campbell's monograph, *Honor, Shame, and the Rhetoric of 1 Peter* (1998), which unites social-scientific and classical rhetorical investigation. Drawing from the social sciences, Campbell situates the epistle within an agonistic honor/shame framework, according to which human interactions are structured around the dominant goal of gaining honor and avoiding shame (Campbell 1998: 12; Malina and Neyrey 1991). Drawing from the classical rhetorical handbooks, Campbell identifies 1 Peter as a piece of *deliberative* rhetoric, meant to exhort an "insider" Christian community whose honor has been threatened by "outsider" non-Christians to behave in certain ways in the future. Campbell organizes the letter according to the traditional rhetorical categories of an *exordium* (introduction; 1:3–12), three distinct *argumentatios* (arguments; 1:13–2:10; 2:11–3:12; 3:13–4:11), and a *peroration* (conclusion; 4:12–5:14), and describes Peter's uses of specific classical rhetorical figures (microrhetoric) in each section.

There are, of course, many classical rhetorical figures in 1 Peter. Let me offer just one example to illustrate: In 1 Peter 2:19–20, Peter employs (also called *erōtēsis eperōtēsis*), or what English speakers today call a "rhetorical question." Aristotle defines *erōtēsis* as a means of summarizing what has gone before in an argument (*Rhet.* 3.19.5), and Quintilian similarly emphasizes that such questions are asked in order to reiterate a prior statement, not because the speaker actually wants new information (*Inst.* 9.2.6–11). Peter begins 2:19 with a declarative statement: "For it is a credit to you if, being aware of God, you endure pain while suffering unjustly"; he then poses a question in order to recapitulate his point: "If you endure when you are beaten for doing wrong, what credit is that?" (2:20). The unspoken implied answer is "no credit at all." He follows up by repeating his earlier claim in positive terms: "But if you endure when you do right and suffer for it, you have God's approval." The question in v. 20 works rhetorically to invoke an answer that subtly reaffirms the author's prior claim.

On the level of macro-rhetoric, scholars have brought a hermeneutic of suspicion to 1 Peter, "reading against the grain" of the Petrine text in order to uncover the voices it most likely works to marginalize. Schüssler Fiorenza's 2017 volume, *1 Peter: An Introduction and Study Guide: Reading against the Grain*, explores how Petrine rhetoric serves existing power structures and silences alternative views. Schüssler Fiorenza also reads scholarly rhetoric *about* 1 Peter through a metacritical lens, critiquing traditional "malestream" scholarship for repeating Peter's rhetoric without critically assessing its ethical implications. According to Schüssler Fiorenza, this purportedly "objectivist" and "depoliticized" scholarship reinscribes oppressive ancient views. Echoing her 1988 SBL address (discussed above), Schüssler Fiorenza calls instead for a "feminist emancipatory, radically democratic" approach to 1 Peter that seeks not only to examine the rhetoric of the epistle, but ultimately to challenge injustices in both ancient and modern scholarly discourse.

Three representatives of the kind of critical engagement that Schüssler Fiorenza commends (though none is cited by Schüssler Fiorenza) are Jennifer Bird, Kathleen Corley, and Halvor Moxnes (Moxnes 2014; Bird 2013; Corley 1994). In their own ways, Moxnes, Bird, and Corley all adopt a hermeneutic of suspicion, emphasizing the problematic ethical implications of 1 Peter's injunctions for women and enslaved people not to retaliate in the face of persecution.[21] Corley, for example, considering Peter's instructions for enslaved people to submit to "perverse" masters, enduring "pain" while "being beaten" and "abused" (2:18–23), underscores the many ways that "Greco-Roman masters could be harsh in their punishments," arguing that "male and female slaves are thus being told to suffer even physical punishment or rape" (Corley 1994: 353). Bird interrogates the household code's "primary dynamic" of "subordination of women to men," as indicative of an entire system based on subordination and domination; this system, which is "defined by male-centered realities," effaces women's experiences and fundamentally limits their participation in the Christian movement to "circumscribed conditions and roles" (Bird 2013: 139). Moxnes writes that while 1 Pet. 2:18–25 is complicit in slavery's "effacement of

---

21   On adding men to the list of victims of Petrine rhetoric, see Visser 2017.

women/non-men," it also paradoxically creates a "space of alterity to that of the slave society" by creating a new kind of subjectivity within it (Moxnes 2014: 135, 138; Moxnes builds on Grosz 1994). Corley, Bird, and Moxnes all ground their analyses of Petrine rhetoric in the first-century CE historical backgrounds in which the text originated, but with added sensitivity to the ethical consequences of that rhetoric for both the intended and unintended audiences who have been influenced by it.

In my own analysis of 1 Peter below, I build on these discussions and weave together several modes of rhetorical study in order to illuminate the Petrine rhetoric of suffering. Specifically, I argue that Peter draws on two sets of rhetorical resources that are rarely brought together in discussions of this epistle's perspectives on suffering: namely, Jewish apocalyptic thought and the rhetoric of exemplarity. Commentaries typically mention suffering, Jewish apocalypticism, and exemplarity separately, recognizing each as a prominent Petrine theme, but few interpreters have read them together from a rhetorical-critical standpoint.

3.3   *First Peter as Jewish Apocalyptic Discourse*

Most scholarship on Jewish apocalyptic literature focuses on the genre of the literary "apocalypse," which typically recounts a privileged seer's visions of the end times in narrative form.[22] Obviously, 1 Peter does not fit this category; it is an epistle composed of overt didactic instruction and direct address. It does, however, constitute apocalyptic discourse, defined by Greg Carey as a "constellation of apocalyptic topics," which functioned as "a flexible set of resources that early Jews and Christians could employ for a variety of persuasive tasks" (Carey 2005: 5). Indeed, the Petrine epistle is permeated by Jewish apocalyptic *topoi*.[23] The letter highlights the trauma of exile and alienation; exhortations to specific action; consolation in the midst of eschatological crises;[24] suffering as a form of testing (note the associations of *lupeō*, "to suffer," and *dokimazō*, "to test," with apocalyptic concepts in 1 Pet. 1:6–7; see, similarly, e.g., Jn. 16:20; 1 Cor. 3:13);[25] and impending eschatological salvation and judgment, including

---

22   See the standard definition of the apocalyptic genre in Collins 1979: 9 and the two additions in Collins 1986: 7.

23   Discussions of 1 Peter's apocalyptic themes include Webb 2007; VanderKam 1996: 62–63; Achtemeier 1996, esp. 105–7; Hays 1989.

24   On apocalyptic literature offering consolation in response to eschatological crises, see, e.g., Collins 2000: esp. 259; Hellholm 1986: esp. 27; more generally, see Holloway 2009: esp. 76–112; Cook 1995.

25   This concept long predates the Petrine letter and Second Temple Judaism. For Plato, suffering tests one's character (*Republic* 413D–E; 503A), while Stoics like Seneca compared

vindication for unjust treatment.[26] There can be no doubt that 1 Peter reflects a Jewish apocalyptic imagination, working rhetorically "to shape [its recipients'] imaginative perception of a situation and so lay the basis for whatever course of action it exhorts" (Collins 1998: 42). The focus on suffering is one of the strongest strands of Jewish apocalyptic tradition to be found in the letter.[27] In spite of the readily-recognized themes just discussed, scholars typically have not treated the rhetoric of suffering in 1 Peter within a Jewish apocalyptic framework.[28]

In one sense, the inattention to the rhetoric of 1 Peter's apocalyptic dimensions reflects the state of the field more broadly. As recently as 2014, Newsom could describe rhetorical criticism of early Jewish and Christian apocalyptic literature as a "young and unformed" subfield (Newsom 2014: 202). This is unfortunate and ought to be remedied. As Newsom insists, even when apocalyptic literature does not "overtly foreground persuasion," it does "construct a symbolic world that makes claims about the nature of reality, constructs highly desirable symbolic objects, invites readers to identify with its representative figures and values, and oftentimes envisions a social world in which identification and division are sharply figured" (Newsom 2014: 203). It is therefore worth asking how 1 Peter, like other Jewish apocalyptic literature, works rhetorically to construct a symbolic world that makes claims on its readers.

One of the most salient rhetorical strategies Peter uses is *exemplarity*, which functions in a number of different ways in the letter.

3.4   *Exemplarity in First Peter*

Repeatedly, Peter draws on *exempla*, or examples, to make his case. He also valorizes exemplarity itself, urging readers to follow the example of those who

---

suffering to parental discipline (*On Providence* 1.5; 2.5–6). See also the survey on suffering as divine discipline in ancient Judaism provided in Sanders 1955: 7–21. For a discussion of suffering as a means of growth in 1 Peter, see Dryden 2006: 44.

26   On the eschatological dimension of 1 Peter's discussion of suffering and resonances with apocalyptic Jewish literature, see Dubis 2002 and Liebengood 2014.

27   The terms most commonly employed for suffering in Jewish apocalyptic literature, *thlipsis/thlibō* ("oppression/affliction") and *diōgmos/diōkō*, do not appear in 1 Peter, with only one exception (*diōkō* appears in 1 Pet. 3:11, but it refers there to pursuing peace). Perhaps it is significant that Peter's term *peirasmos* (1 Pet. 1:6; 4:12) *is* associated with *thlipsis* and *diōgmos* elsewhere in NT literature (e.g., Matt. 13:21; 1 Thess. 3:4; Rev. 2:10), or that the Petrine language of foreignness and alienation also appears in other apocalyptic literature (e.g., CD VI.5; 1QS VIII.U3; 1QpHab XI.6; 1QM I2; additional parallels between 1 Peter and specific Jewish apocalypses are readily accessible elsewhere). Ultimately, however, the absence of specific vocabulary is not sufficient justification for ignoring how 1 Peter's depictions of suffering are rooted in Jewish apocalyptic thought.

28   One exception is Holdsworth 1980.

have gone before, most especially, Christ, who "suffered for you, leaving you an example, so that you should follow in his steps" (2:21). It is easy to assume that such examples function plainly, as straightforward illustrations or calls to imitation. However, exemplarity is actually quite complex. The logic animating each case of exemplarity differs, and the rhetorical functions and effects of examples differ depending on how or whether their recipients (attempt to) emulate them. Furthermore, as I will delineate below, in 1 Peter, the rhetoric of exemplarity is multi-layered, contributing to the Petrine persuasive agenda on both "micro" levels (i.e., conventions, figures, grammatical constructions, etc.) and "macro" levels (i.e., themes, concepts, ideas, etc.). Exemplification raises a nexus of interconnected and complicated questions concerning 1 Peter's rhetoricity, none of which has been adequately theorized in New Testament studies.

My aim in the following discussion is twofold: The first is to read Peter's references to suffering within a Jewish apocalyptic context. The second is to explore how, within that context, Peter employs examples strategically in the text (micro-rhetoric) in order to present suffering as its own form of exemplarity (macro-rhetoric). I shall then present a brief case study, in which I argue that Peter uses the so-called "household code" (commonly called a *Haustafel*) in 1 Pet. 2:13–3:7 as a potent paradigmatic appeal regarding proper Christian responses to apocalyptic suffering. The advice therein has most commonly been read as applicable only to each specific category addressed (first, enslaved people, then wives, then husbands). I contend, in contrast, that all of the examples—individual named figures like Christ and Sarah *and* the general categories—together bolster Peter's claims elsewhere that leading an exemplary Christian life will engender suffering, but that this suffering should be borne because it is both evangelistically effective and temporary.

We begin by looking at how 1 Peter imbues Christian suffering with "an apocalyptic flavor" by participating in the Jewish apocalyptic discourse of the Second Temple era (Liebengood 2014: 116).

3.5   *Reading First Peter's Rhetoric of Suffering in a Jewish Apocalyptic Framework*

1 Peter draws on a number of familiar Jewish apocalyptic *topoi* in its depiction of suffering. First, suffering is portrayed as a temporary feature of the present eschatological crisis. Divine vindication is not only promised (e.g., 1:5–7, 12–13, 20; 5:1), but imminent, since "the end of all things is near" (*pantōn de to telos ēggiken*, 4:7). Indeed, a recurring motif in 1 Peter is the juxtaposition of the relative brevity of earthly suffering with the eternal glory that is to come, when Christ's eternal glory will be revealed and shared. Christians are suffering "now, for a short time" (*oligon arti*, 1:6; *oligos* appears also in 3:20; 5:10, 12), but they will be relieved "in the apocalypse/revelation of [Christ's] glory"

(*tēs doxēs*, 4:13). Christians, having "suffered for a little while" (*oligon pathontas*) as those called to "eternal glory in Christ" (*tēn aiōnion autou doxan*, 5:10), will themselves receive "the unfading crown of glory (*doxēs*)" (5:4). Peter describes the prophets as glorified witnesses who "testified beforehand to the sufferings (*pathēmata*) destined for Christ and the subsequent glory (*doxēs*)" (1:11); he later identifies himself in parallel fashion as a witness of Christ's sufferings who also will partake in the future glory (*doxēs*) that is to be revealed (5:1).

Second, 1 Peter presupposes that suffering will be corporeal. Repeatedly, Christ's suffering is defined in bodily terms: Christians are called to follow Christ, who "suffered in the flesh" (*pathontos sarki*) and was ultimately "put to death in the flesh" (*thanatōtheis sarki*, 3:18), since "the one who suffers in the flesh" (*ho pathōn sarki*) has finished with sin (4:1). The assumption that fleshly abuse and physical suffering are inevitable contrasts with the rhetoric we find elsewhere in ancient literature. Other contemporaneous groups, such as the Hellenistic therapeutic dream cults, taught that after performing proper rituals, sufferers would experience physical healing. A defining feature of Jewish and Christian apocalyptic discourse is that promises of physical well-being are "replaced by psychological consolation" (Flannery 2014: 110; on cathartic functions of apocalyptic literature, see Collins 1984). References to "psychological consolation," however, ought not obscure the stark brutality that attends Petrine calls for the enslaved and other oppressed people to emulate Christ by submitting to physical abuse without retaliating. As elsewhere in apocalyptic literature, the temporary (*oligos*) nature of earthly suffering and promised eternal glory (*doxa*) fail to mitigate the severity of the suffering to which readers are called.

Third, apocalyptic suffering in 1 Peter is not *only* physical; it is also relational, or interpersonal. According to Peter, suffering is "unjustly" (*adikōs*, 2:19) imposed on God's people by "the Gentiles/nations" (*tōn ethnōn*, 2:12; 4:3). Both elements are significant: the Christian suffers "as a Christian" (*hōs Christianos*, 4:16), and the Christian suffers *at the hands of* non-Christians. Peter says his recipients suffer "for their righteousness" (*dia dikaiosunēn*, 3:14). In his examples of this Christian suffering, Peter employs verbs of slander (e.g., *katalaleō*, 2:12; *oneidizō*, 4:14) to depict Christians suffering as the object of others' suspicion and derision. 1 Pet. 4:3–4 refers to the letter's recipients withdrawing from certain social activities:

> You have already spent enough time in doing what the Gentiles like to do, living in licentiousness, passions, drunkenness, revels, carousing, and lawless idolatry. They are surprised that you no longer join them in the same excesses of debauchery, and so they blaspheme.

Williams argues that Christians were voluntarily disassociating from former social alliances such as the imperial cult, while Holloway explains the withdrawal as the consequence of others stigmatizing them (Williams 2012: 240–58; Holloway 2009: esp. 125, 128, 212; cf. Bechtler 1998: 69). Scholars who read from a social-scientific perspective have argued that 1 Peter's preoccupation with hostile social encounters between Christians and non-Christians indicates that early Christians had actually lost their honor in an honor/shame-based culture (Campbell 1998). According to these reconstructions, Christians suffered from a "ubiquitous and constant" prejudice (Holloway 2009: 2), and/or they endured a "mocking" and "pejorative" attitude from "outsiders" (Trebilco 2004: 554–56). Elliott contends that they faced a "barrage of verbal abuse designed to shame, defame, demean, and discredit [them] as social and moral deviants" (2007: 78).

Rhetorical analysis turns our critical spotlight from questions about whether Christians *actually chose* to self-segregate and questions about how non-Christians *actually were* treating Christians to the persuasive impact of Peter's claims about Christian and non-Christian interactions. Rhetoric, Burke observes, reveals "the ways in which individuals are at odds with one another, or become identified with groups more or less at odds with one another" (Burke 1969: 22). Regardless of whether non-Christians *actually* discriminated against Christians and caused them to suffer, what matters from a rhetorical perspective is that 1 Peter *describes* them doing so. For example, Peter repeatedly uses the same root word, "righteous(ness)" (*dikaios, dikaiosunē*), to juxtapose the injustice (*adikaios*) of non-Christians with the righteousness of those who follow Christ (2:19, 23, 24; 3:12, 14, 18; 4:18). The language itself creates and solidifies the group identity of righteous Christians over and against the unrighteousness of others.

One rhetorical effect of such depictions may have been increased communal solidarity amongst Christians who perceived themselves as rejected and misunderstood by others. Picking up another *topos* that appears commonly in apocalyptic literature, the epistle employs the combined language of election and chosen peoplehood to refer to a suffering minoritized group.[29] Just as Christ was "rejected by humans, yet chosen by and precious to God" (2:4), so too, are Peter's recipients "called to inherit a blessing" (3:9). They are chosen to "be built" into a "spiritual house, a holy priesthood" (2:5). Peter refers to those who follow the example of Jesus as the "elect" or "chosen race" (2:9), a "holy *ethnos*" (2:9) who were "once not a people" (2:10), but are "now the people of

---

29   For illuminating treatments of the ethnic/racial dimensions of early Christian claims to be a "new *genos* (people/race)," see Buell 2005 and Horrell 2011.

God" (2:10). This vision of a community of chosen "believers" (*tois pisteuousin*) is opposed to (and in this way, creates the impression of) a mirror-image community of "unbelievers" (*apistousin*, 2:7). The Petrine use of the exile motif contributes to this dichotomizing insofar as the emphasis is not on exile itself, but on Christians suffering *together* (*sumpatheis*, 3:8, a *hapax legomenon* in the New Testament). Peter insists, "above all" (*pro pantōn*), that Christians should keep constant in their love for each other (4:8), because Christians everywhere experience "the same kinds of suffering" (5:9).

Whether Christians were voluntarily refraining from certain groups and behaviors or being unwillingly excluded by others, rhetorically, 1 Peter paints a picture of Christians refraining, i.e., "no longer joining," together, that is, *as a group*. Set over and against a hostile culture of unbelievers, the shared sufferings of Christ's followers are rhetorically alchemized into a source of communal strength. In this way, Peter's rhetoric of a suffering community contributes to the creation of that very community.

Peter's community-differentiating persuasive tactics function not only on the level of themes and ideas (macro-rhetoric), but also on the level of grammar and sentence patterns (micro-rhetoric). Recall the example of classical rhetorical conventions presented above: Peter's strategic use of rhetorical questions. Peter employs rhetorical questions differently in various parts of the letter. As I already mentioned, in 1 Pet. 2:20, Peter poses a rhetorical question in order to recapitulate an earlier assertion ("If you endure when you are beaten for doing wrong, what credit is that?"). Two chapters later, Peter employs rhetorical questions again, but here, they function as a means of aligning Peter's audience with a particular in-group and opposing them to a circumscribed group of outsiders. He first says: "For the time has come for judgment to begin with the household (*oikos*) of God" (4:17a). He then immediately asks a question that simultaneously associates himself and his audience ("us") with those within the "household of God," and differentiates them from the disobedient ones, who are not within God's *oikos*: "If it [judgment] begins with us, what will be the end for those who do not obey (*apeithountōn*) the gospel of God?" (4:17b) After situating his readers over and against those who disobey God, Peter reinforces that identification with yet another rhetorical question. This one is a citation from the book of Proverbs, a Scriptural text that his readers presumably already take to be authoritative: "If it is hard for the righteous to be saved, what will become of the ungodly and the sinner?" (4:18; LXX Prov. 11:31) Peter leaves the questions in 4:17–18 unanswered because the answers themselves are not the point; the next word, "therefore" (*hōste*, 4:19), solidifies this sense that the rhetorical work performed by the questions is far more important for Peter's argument than the answers. The persuasive function of the rhetorical questions in ch. 4 is to encourage the in-group, "the suffering ones," to "entrust their souls to a faithful Creator, while continuing to do good" together, as a community (4:19).

To summarize this section thus far: Like other Jewish apocalyptic discourses, 1 Peter depicts suffering as: 1) temporary, paling in comparison with eternal glory; 2) bodily and potentially severe for those lower in a patriarchal system; and 3) unjustly imposed by outsiders onto innocent insiders. 1 Peter thus puts early Christian sufferings to good rhetorical use, employing elements of Jewish apocalyptic discourse to transform Christians' perceived struggles into a beneficial defining feature of the inchoate community of Christ followers.

What responses does the letter advocate in the face of such suffering?

Peter admonishes his readers to respond to suffering by rejoicing and being glad (1:6, 8; 4:13), glorifying God (4:11, 16) because they are "sharing in the sufferings of Christ" (*koinōneite tois tou Christou pathēmasin*, 4:13). Much of the critical discussion of Peter's advice to endure suffering without retaliating (on which, Schertz 1992: esp. 283–85) has focused on his recipients' precarious status as a minority group in the Roman Empire: Is Peter arguing that Jesus followers ought to display "publicly conformist and submissive behavior" (Carter 2004: 28), or is his advice actually counter-cultural and "quite revolutionary" (Campbell 1998: 151; recently, see Le Roux 2019)? This debate is often described in shorthand as the "Balch-Elliott debate," referring to two prominent interlocutors on the topic, David Balch and John Elliott, both of whom published monographs in 1981 and interacted with one another in several publications thereafter (e.g., Balch 1986; Elliott 1986). Although Balch and Elliott themselves mount nuanced arguments, the unfortunate result of the familiar either/or formulation is that the early Christian experience "becomes narrowly confined to two options: accommodation or resistance." In reality, early Christians' interactions with and responses to the Roman Empire were far more variegated (Williams 2014: 139).

Both positions—i.e., accommodation and resistance—share an underlying assumption that scholars have rarely acknowledged or explored: namely, both assume the value of exemplarity vis-à-vis the surrounding culture. Whether the purported goal is for non-Christians to view Christians as non-threatening to Roman power, or to challenge the dominant order (however subtly), both positions presuppose that Peter's goal is to persuade his readers to exemplify certain behaviors and thereby manage others' perceptions of them. Few interpreters have given much critical attention to the ways that Peter's endorsement of certain behaviors, and his uses of Christ's and others' examples, participate in broader rhetorical discourses about exemplarity in the ancient world.

It is worth pausing for a moment to consider how exemplarity was discussed and used in antiquity.

3.6   *Rhetoric(s) of Exemplarity in the Ancient World*

Writers throughout the ancient world were keenly aware of exemplarity's power to influence an audience; belief in this persuasive power is evident across various genres and settings in ancient literature. In the classical rhetorical handbooks and treatises on rhetoric, exemplarity is considered an effective means of honing writers' and orators' persuasive practices (MacDonald 2001). The pedagogical import of *mimēsis* (Greek) and its Latin equivalent, *imitatio*, was valued in rhetorical training, as rhetoricians advised students to copy prior examples of laudatory literary styles and strategies, and often provided such examples in their handbooks (e.g., Cicero, *De Or.* 2.87–97; Dionysius of Halicarnassus's *Peri mimeseos*; on *exempla* in Roman pedagogy, see the classic Marrou 1956, esp. 230–77).

Rhetorical theorists also discussed *exempla* as useful strategies for transforming readers "through the process of emulation—into someone else, someone better" (Langlands 2018: 2). Historical *exempla*, for instance, are persuasive, Aristotle explains, "because as a rule the future resembles the past" (*Ars Rhet.* 2.20.8). Similarly, Cicero declares that a reference to an historical *exemplum* "supports or weakens a case by appeal to precedent or experience" (*De Inv.* 1.30.49); elsewhere, he praises the past as a "storehouse of examples and precedents," and records Antonius calling history "the teacher of our lives" (*De Or.* 1.18, 2.36). Historiographers such as Polybius, Herodotus, and Thucydides used history as "a source of education, learning, civilisation, and an inexhaustible reservoir of moral examples," albeit in different ways (Enenkel 2001: 75).[30] Livy, for one, presents accounts of courageous fighting in battle as a means of inspiring courage in others: "If so many examples of courage did not inspire you, nothing ever will" (*Hist.* 22.60.14). Roman moralists similarly collected stories of Roman heroes as a means of imparting ethical advice and inculcating virtue in their readers. Valerius Maximus's *Facta et Dicta Memorabilia* offers nearly a thousand exempla, from which, he writes, "the human race is nourished and augmented" (5.2.ext.4; see also, e.g., Quintilian's famous list of role models in *Inst.* 10.1–2).

Examples are used for explanatory, inspirational, and transformative purposes throughout early Christian and ancient Jewish literature, as well. In the Gospels, Jesus uses examples such as similes, parables, and allegories to describe what the kingdom of heaven "is like" (e.g., Matt. 13:24), to discourage or

---

30   See also, e.g., Petitfils 2016; Hau 2016; Price 1975.

encourage certain behaviors (e.g., Lk. 4:25–27; 7:44–46), and to explain his own identity metaphorically (e.g., Jn. 6:35; 8:12). He also repeatedly presents himself as a model to emulate, calling his hearers to "follow" him (e.g., Matt. 8:22; 16:24; Mk. 10:21; Lk. 9:59; Jn. 1:43; 10:27; 21:19). In the Pauline epistles, we read that Adam is "a figure/type (*tupos*) of the one to come" (Rom. 5:14) and that Jerusalem typifies the church (e.g., Gal. 4:25–26). The writer of Hebrews calls Christ a priest "like Melchizedek" (Heb. 5:5–10; 6:20; 7:1–17) and famously lists Jewish ancestors as exemplary predecessors for readers to emulate (Heb. 11; on Christian uses of historical *exempla* from the Hebrew Bible, see Eisenbaum 1997; on ancient Jewish and Christian moral discourses of exemplarity, see Petitfils 2015). Second Temple Jewish literature often points to historical exemplars as models for the behavior it commends; Josephus, for instance, depicts Joseph as the epitome of modesty and chastity (*Antiquities* 4). Philo, for his part, expressly declares that he is writing the life of Moses because unlike the Greeks, who waste their education on writing comedies, he wishes to "preserv[e] a record of virtuous men and praiseworthy lives" (*Moses* 1.3). And exemplarity plays a major role in Jewish discourse beyond the Second Temple period; as Daniel Boyarin and others have demonstrated, "exemplification was one of the most significant modes of expression in rabbinic thought," as well (Boyarin 1995: 31).

Countless other examples of exemplification could be adduced from the texts of antiquity because the conviction was pervasive: Examples are rhetorically effective and useful in many and varied contexts, for many and varied persuasive ends.

Still, the view *that* exemplarity is influential does not explain *how* exemplarity influences, let alone how examples influence via texts. The ubiquity and flexibility of examples in literature can lead us to assume that they function in a straightforward manner, as though an author presents an example, its import is clear, and its audience subsequently re-creates the original in their own lives. New Testament scholars' propensity for etymological explanations fuels that impression. Commentators frequently note that *tupos* derives from the Greek verb *tupoō* ("to stamp," "to impress a mark"), which evokes the image of stamping a mark or picture unchanged onto a coin. Aristotle's *paradeigma* ("model," "paradigm"), which derives from the Greek verb *paradeiknumi* ("to exhibit side by side," "to compare"), similarly establishes a clear horizontal relationship between original and copy, past and present.[31]

---

31   Well-known works on this in the field of rhetorical studies include Benoit 1980, 1987 and McGuire 1982.

Examples seem to make inherent sense to us. Nevertheless, examples only seem to be simple. Scholars in modern rhetorical studies and in the field of Classics have drawn attention to a dual ontology underlying exemplarity. On the one hand, examples that function like the Aristotelian *paradeigma* present one instance that *typifies* an overarching category, as a robin might exemplify the category "bird." On the other hand, examples can also function like the Latin *exemplum*, which is the opposite of a *paradeigma*. *Exemplum* stems from the verb *eximere* ("to cut out," "to subtract"); thus, it is an exception, something *set apart* from a group. A writer or speaker might present an example in the first mode as something that typifies a general category, like when Jesus uses the Pharisees and teachers of the law to exemplify the broader category of "hypocrites" (Matt. 23:27). Or one can use an example in the second mode as something unique that hearers should emulate but can never truly copy, like when Paul tells his readers to "be imitators (*mimētai*) of God" (Eph. 5:1). As Matthew Roller observes, these two sides of exemplarity are often described separately as "illustrative" (*paradeigma*) and "injunctive" (*exemplum*), but "in practice the two modes often intermingle" (Roller 2018: 52).

This dual ontology problematizes simplistic notions of literary exemplarity's rhetoricity. How does a rhetor's presentation of an example as illustrative or injunctive—or perhaps an intermingling of the two—impact its communicative power? How do readerly preconceptions shape the reception of examples? Can *exempla* inculcate beliefs and behaviors in reliably generalizable ways, or is each example inextricably wedded to the (textual, contextual, extratextual) particulars in which it is embedded? Must *exempla* teach about something—say, a virtue—that typifies a category or concept with which one is *already* familiar, or can examples establish new *gnosis*, fresh understanding of lessons previously unknown?

Literary exemplarity is further complicated when the example adduced comes from a past written text (and not just from an author's account of an unwritten past). How, then, does exemplarity relate to intertextuality? As Julia Kristeva has famously explained, intertextuality consists of more than mere citation or repetition; texts *transform* one another (Kristeva 1980: 37). If this is so, and if, as noted above, exemplarity is used to *transform* readers, then we might ask: How does an intertextually-transformed example work to transform readers? Must an audience know and/or already acknowledge the authority of a prior written text for an intertextual example to be persuasive? Layers pile on interpretive layers: How does (or should) the rhetor's interpretation of a prior exemplary text influence his audience's interpretation of *his* interpretation?

While rhetoricians like Cicero may have lauded exact imitation of human or literary figures as an ideal, their discussions betray a more flexible understanding of exemplarity. Recognizing there is more to imitation than simply creating an exact replica or copy of a prior type, ancient rhetoricians allowed for—indeed, they encouraged—revisions of *exempla* in order to fit the exigencies of particular contexts. Not only that, but they recognized that this malleability complicated the reception and interpretation of *exempla*. In an important recent study of Roman exemplary tales, Langlands traces how the stories themselves exhibit "sensitivity to the difficulties of interpreting exemplary deeds [and] awareness of situational variability, whereby virtues must be enacted differently depending on the circumstances" (Langlands 2018: 4). Ancient writers knew that the persuasiveness of any given example depends on an audience's prior knowledge and present situation (e.g., Quintilian, *Inst. Or.* 5.11.6–16).

Exemplarity in literary texts gives rise not to certainty, but to persuasive potentiality. Literary scholar Timothy Hampton suggests that we ought to think of exemplarity in terms of paradoxical juxtapositions. A literary evocation of a past exemplar is "a kind of textual node or point of juncture," at which universality and particularity, hermeneutical procedures and rhetorical desires, appropriations of the past and commended responses to the present all come together in an attempt to influence readers (Hampton 1990: 3).[32] Hampton's explanation is worth citing at length:

> [T]he evocation of the exemplary ... makes a claim on the reader's action in the world. Allusion to the virtuous or heroic model sets up an implicit moral comparison between [present] reader and ancient exemplar ... [and] constitutes that textual moment at which the authority of the past is brought to bear on the reader's response to the text. The exemplar [is] where a given author's interpretation of the past overlaps with the desire to form and fashion readers ... in the representation of exemplary figures the hermeneutic procedures through which [a particular] culture has appropriated the texts and actors of the past interface with the rhetorical procedures through which [certain] texts fashion the responses of their own readers.
>
> HAMPTON 1990: 3

A literary exemplar brings the past to bear on the present and future. It constitutes the textual moment at which an author implicitly invokes authority over his audience's future by presenting his own hermeneutical appropriations of

---

32   Hampton focuses on Renaissance literature; though he works with a different literary corpus, his insights apply to the rhetorical functions of *exempla* in ancient literature, as well.

an authoritative past. Importantly, authors cannot simply present an example as it existed objectively in the past; they can only offer their construal of that past example. In this sense, literary exemplarity constitutes a forming and fashioning of the past for the purpose of forming and fashioning an audience's future.

A literary exemplar also paradoxically draws together the universal and the unique. From a rhetorical perspective, authors use examples to address a perceived exigence. A kind of assumed collectivity undergirds this rhetorical move, insofar as authors expect both that the exigence will be shared by their intended recipients, and that the example adduced will be efficacious in the context of that exigence. At the same time, exemplarity is not only the point where universality inheres; it is also the point at which the conceptual wall between commonality and distinctiveness breaks down. Universality and particularity must come together if they are to constitute a meaningful claim on a particular audience, since every act of understanding—and therefore, every act of influence—is mediated by the historically-shaped structures of specific cultures and contexts. Exemplarity's value, writes Derrida, is that it "inscribes the universal in the proper body of a singularity, of an idiom or culture, whether this singularity be individual, social, national, state, federal, confederal, or not" (Derrida 1992: 72).

Exemplarity also unites the singular with the social. Analyzing Roman uses of historical *exempla* to inculcate proper Roman morality, Roller describes exemplarity as a form of "social reproduction": Individual heroes embody positive Roman attributes such as *virtus* and *pietas* (and vices to avoid), monuments are erected to commemorate them, new spectators witness and emulate illustrious actions, and so "deeds generate other deeds, spawning ever more audiences and monuments, in an endless loop of social reproduction" (2004: 6). Though Roller focuses on a specific tradition of Roman morality discourse, the "cyclical dimension" that he identifies works analogously with other rhetorical uses of exempla, such as those we find in biblical literature.

The problem, of course, what Gelley refers to as "the scandal of example," is that these processes of social reproduction can go awry (Gelley 1995: 14). Examples are "unruly" (Gelley 1995). What's more, texts that are transmitted out in the world become disconnected from and elude authorial control. The reasons that an author praises a particular example, or the ways in which an audience is being enjoined to emulate that example, may not be clear to (all) readers. Langlands argues that this indeterminacy is one source of exemplarity's cultural power, since the contestable nature of examples can provoke critical thought, dispute, and dialogue amongst audiences (Langlands 2015; 2018). To this, I would add that even when an exemplar's claim on readers *is* clear, responses to such claims will vary. An example presented is not inevitably an example imitated, or imitated exactly. To be simplistic about it, this is why debates have raged for centuries in the Christian Church over what it might mean to "follow Christ's example." Texts may transform, but they do not transform uniformly or universally.

Returning to 1 Peter, the dual ontology of exemplarity is on full display: Christ's example is like the Latin *exemplum*, something *set apart* that technically cannot be reproduced by his followers (Christ suffered "once," *hapax*, for sins, 3:18). Yet, by entreating Christians to emulate Christ's suffering, Peter also presents it like the Aristotelian *paradeigma*, something that *typifies* a larger category. This larger category continues to typify and replicate itself. Peter's commendations of Christ's suffering are similar to the Roman uses of exemplarity as a form of "social reproduction." A text can be read as its own dynamic monument to exemplary deeds, aimed at generating similar attitudes and actions in its (multiple, multiplying) audiences and thereby not only lauding but reproducing the singular in the social. Peter commemorates Christ's suffering as salvific in order to generate a similar view of suffering in his immediate intended audience, the letter's recipients. Ideally, however, this shared perspective will not stop with Peter's immediate audience.

1 Peter argues that Christians should suffer willingly as a benefit to unbelieving others, since they might win unbelievers to Christ through their holy conduct—in other words, they might gain adherents by their exemplary behavior. Those who "conduct [them]selves honorably among the Gentiles" will silence their critics, but the silencing itself is not the ultimate goal. Christians ought to behave honorably "in order that (*hina*)" unbelievers might join those who "glorify God when he comes to judge" (2:12). Echoing Isaiah 53 ("he was wounded for our transgressions, crushed for our iniquities; upon him was the punishment that made us whole, and by his bruises we are healed," Isa. 53:5), 1 Peter argues that those who suffer "while continuing to do good" (4:19) do so not only because of, but also for the benefit of "the ungodly and the sinners" (4:18). That 1 Peter depicts suffering as simultaneously salutary for Christians (as a united new community) and for unbelievers (as potential future members of that community) is unsurprising in light of the fact, discussed above, that Jewish apocalyptic suffering is interpersonal for Peter; it makes sense that his chosen response would be relationally-oriented, as well.

Linking Christ's original salvific act with the positive reverberating effects of imitating it, 1 Peter's evocations of Christ's suffering are geared toward "spawning ever more audiences and monuments" (Roller 2004: 6). In this case, the monuments obviously are not literal, physical monuments. If they behave as Peter hopes, the audience itself will become the monument—the "living stones" that are "built into a spiritual house" (2:5)—standing as testament to Christ's exemplarity. Suffering thus becomes for Peter its own form of exemplarity, and a potent evangelistic tool for potential converts.

The following section presents a case study—a *paradeigma*—of the household code in 1 Pet. 2:13–3:7. This fascinating passage has spawned much scholarly debate, but it has rarely been read rhetorically in light of the multiple discourses about Jewish apocalypticism, suffering, or exemplarity that we have in view.

3.7   *Case Study: Rhetoric and the Household Code in First Pet. 2:13–3:7*

The Petrine household code stands as a kind of textual monument to the top-down kyriarchal structure of the Roman Empire. Like other discussions of household management from antiquity, 1 Pet. 2:13–3:7 reflects the conviction that order in the *oikoumenē*, or "inhabited world," is rooted in a well-ordered *oikos*, or "household" (in the New Testament, see also Col. 3:18–4:1 and Eph. 5:21–6:9). The ancient *oikos*, importantly, was not like what we associate with the word "household" today; instead of a nuclear family living together in a domestic residence, it was more like a small but bustling economic hub (*oikonomos* is where we get the word "economy"). This centralized mini-economy, which typically included a whole community of free and enslaved people, was overseen by a ruling *kyrios*, or "lord." The household code stipulates how people within such an *oikos* ought to behave. Scholars typically have not read the Petrine household code through the lenses of the discourses we have discussed thus far: The code is rarely seen as Jewish, apocalyptic, or concerned with suffering; quite to the contrary, as we shall see. Neither have the complexities of exemplarity in the code been analyzed.[33] What explains these critical omissions, especially when these topics are so prominent in discussions of the rest of the epistle? I will mention here a few of the reasons, and why I advocate a rhetorical approach instead.

The first reason has to do with chronology: accounts of early Christian history commonly state that over time, the intense eschatological expectations such as those expressed in 1 Thessalonians diminished, and Christians embraced instead the stabilizing effects of the "household code trajectory [that] christianizes patriarchal social and ecclesial structures" (Schüssler Fiorenza 1984: 73).[34] Accordingly, one often finds claims that the Petrine

---

33   One exception to scholars' tendency not to read the household code in a context of suffering is that feminist and postcolonial scholars such as Schüssler Fiorenza, Bird, Corley, and Moxnes (discussed above) have drawn attention to the ways that Peter's instructions may have increased the suffering of women and enslaved people within household hierarchies.

34   Martin Dibelius articulated this view in 1913, and it has been much repeated since.

Haustafel is evidence of the epistle's relatively late date and concomitant shift *away* from the first-century CE apocalyptic worldview displayed in Paul's epistles. Pokorný's articulation is representative:

> The adoption of the household codes *could not yet* have taken place in the era of apocalyptic expectation of an imminent return during which the main letters of Paul were written.
>
> 1991: 177; emphasis added

The assumption that a concern for order and structure cannot be apocalyptic underlies many comparisons between the Pauline and non-Pauline epistles. For instance, Bird, contrasting 1 Peter's concern with wives' adornment in his household code (3:3–4) with the lack of such injunctions in Paul's letters, attributes the absence of such instructions in Paul to his "general apocalyptic urgency." Bird thus implies by contrast that Peter cares about wifely appearance because, for him, apocalyptic urgency has waned (Bird 2013: 96). Reconstructing early Christian development in this way has led many to conclude that the Petrine *Haustafel* reflects an *anti-* or *post*-apocalyptic perspective, or, at the very least, that it bespeaks the writer's conviction that earlier promises of an imminent new age have failed.

However, this view ignores the fact that order is one of the most prominent *topoi* in Jewish apocalyptic literature. Rhetoric asks us to attend to the function of repeated themes, which writers employ in the service of larger persuasive aims. Order is one such theme. As Newsom observes, order "is at the heart of the symbolic imagination of apocalyptic literature and shapes its rhetoric," whether the patterns of order are "cosmological, historical, or moral" (Newsom 2014: 212). It is clear enough historically that as time marched on and communities of Jesus followers accepted a delayed parousia, they organized themselves into churches with ordained leaders and stable hierarchical structures. Still, a concern for order is not in and of itself indicative of an anti- or post-apocalyptic perspective. We ought to ask how 1 Peter 2:13–3:7 functions as a part of the rest of the letter, which is clearly a tightly crafted rhetorical composition of apocalyptic discourse. We shall return to this below.

Another possible reason for scholars' relative reticence to see the Petrine *Haustafel* as a reflection of a Jewish apocalyptic imagination concerns a scholarly project that largely dominated the twentieth century: that is, the source-critical search for the origins of the New Testament *Haustafeln*. Recognizing resonances with other discourses on household management from antiquity, scholars sought to identify the New Testament writers' source texts for the household codes in Colossians, Ephesians, and 1 Peter. The overwhelming tendency in such source-critical endeavors has been to compare the

New Testament *Haustafeln* with similar discussions in non-Jewish Greek and Roman literature. Some detected the most relevant comparanda in Aristotle's *Politics* 1 (e.g., *Pol.* 1.1260a 9–14), which addresses husband-wife, father-child, and master-slave pairings, and the Aristotelian *oikonomia* tradition that developed subsequently (e.g., Lührmann 1980). Martin Dibelius and his student, Karl Weidinger (Dibelius 1926; Weidinger 1926), famously posited that the New Testament *Haustafeln* originated from a branch of Stoic ethics called *kathēkon* ("suitable actions"), identifying parallels with Stoic lists of moral duties within households (e.g., Seneca, *De Beneficiis* Ep. 94.1–2; Epictetus, *Diss.* 2.14.9).[35] More recently, Dryden has read 1 Peter as an example of Greco-Roman *paraenesis* (exhortation toward moral development); for Dryden, the Petrine household code is employed as a paraenetic strategy like those found in other ancient (non-Jewish) paraenetic epistles, such as Isocrates's Letter to Demonicus and Seneca's *Epistulae Morales* (Dryden 2006: 5). Although some scholars have drawn attention to Hellenistic Jewish writers' instructions on household management (Philo, *De Decalogo* 165–67; *De Hypothetica* 7:1–14; Josephus, *Contra Apion* 2.1990; on which, Schroeder 1959; Crouch 1972), the impulse to turn to non-Jewish comparanda remains strong.

As I said in the section on metacritical rhetorical analysis, the state of biblical scholarship is the direct result of the particular ways that scholarly conversations have unfolded over time. The study of rhetoric underscores how the unconscious biases we inherit from our predecessors inevitably influence our methodological processes and our interpretive conclusions. In comparative discussions of the *Haustafeln*, scholars like those just mentioned, who are interested in the codes' origins, tend to focus on *similarities* between the New Testament examples and other household-related discussions from antiquity. In contrast, scholars who are interested in Christianity's distinctive elements typically highlight the *differences* between Christian and non-Christian discussions of household management. For example, unlike other ancient *Haustafeln*, the New Testament codes address oppressed groups like women and slaves directly as active agents. The New Testament codes also subject *all* members of the household to Christ as *kyrios*. These are potentially revolutionary moves when contrasted with standard kyriarchal norms that privileged the elite male *paterfamilias*, who owned the others as his property. Whether due to an emphasis on parallels to non-Jewish Greco-Roman texts, or because of a focus on the distinctively Christian elements of the New Testament codes, the

---

35   On the Christianization of Seneca and other Hellenistic thinkers in the early church, see Malherbe 1992: 269–70.

scholarly inclination to read the Petrine household code as something *other than* Jewish apocalyptic discourse has persisted.

The search for the origins of the *Haustafeln* also explains, in part, why so few scholars have read 1 Pet. 2:13–3:7 rhetorically through the lens of exemplarity. Indeed, it is ironic that the scholarly preoccupation with one kind of exemplarity—i.e., the fact that New Testament *Haustafeln* appear to be imitations of other ancient household codes—has contributed to the neglect of another form of exemplarity—viz., the rhetorical uses of examples within the passage. For what else is a household code, if not a list of examples? The passage is packed full of them: Peter refers to the emperor and governors as examples of authoritative human institutions (2:13–14), and presents Christ as the ultimate *hupogrammos* that Christians should follow (2:21). He directly addresses slaves (2:18), wives (3:1), and husbands (3:7)—all of whom exemplify different status rankings within a typical ancient household hierarchy. Within the address to wives, Peter appeals to the example of the "holy women" of "long ago" (3:5), specifically naming the Jewish matriarch Sarah as one of them (3:6). Yet, few have asked how exemplarity functions rhetorically in this passage.

1 Pet. 2:21–25 *has* regularly been read in light of exemplarity, though in a different sense than the rhetoric of exemplarity discussed above. Mainly, treatments of Christ's example have focused on the related theological concerns of salvation and discipleship. Peter uses the word *hupogrammos* (lit.: "under-writing") to describe Christ's example: "For to this [enduring in suffering] you have been called, because Christ also suffered for you, leaving you an example (*hupogrammos*), so that you should follow in his steps" (2:21). *Hupogrammos*, a *hapax legomenon* in the New Testament, usually refers to the copy of the alphabet that students make when learning their letters; as such, it functions as a "'guiding image' that is more than an example freely chosen; it puts one under obligation" (Moxnes 2014: 137). Later in the letter, Peter is careful to specify that Christ's suffering alone is eschatologically *salvific*: "Because Christ suffered *once (hapax)* for sins ... in order to bring you to God" (3:18). Those who adopt Christ's "same intention" to suffer have "finished with sin" (4:1) because suffering reorients desire and changes behavior (4:2–4). Some critics have situated Peter's use of Christ's example within the well-known ancient philosophical tradition of moral exhortation (e.g., Malherbe 1986), while others have discussed Petrine exhortations to holiness as a part of the theological tradition commonly called the *imitatio Dei* (and relatedly, the *imitatio Christi*; e.g., Capes 2003). Either way, an irony again presents itself: interpreters' focus on exemplarity in one sense—namely, Christ's uniquely salvific suffering and its consequent call for discipleship as the means to salvation—has led them to disregard exemplarity in a different sense—i.e., how exemplarity works in

and through the household code as an integrated aspect of the epistle's larger rhetorical project.

The third and final reason I wish to highlight that scholars do not usually read the Petrine household code as Jewish apocalyptic discourse, or as concerned with suffering or exemplarity, stems from traditional methods of New Testament exegesis. New Testament scholars, aiming for total breadth and depth in their analyses, often focus on such small bits of text that they lose the forest for the trees. Entire scholarly monographs about one word or phrase may provide good fodder for jokes about academia's myopia, but they are understandable given reigning expectations that *real* scholarship is thorough, precise, and absolutely comprehensive. Ironically, Herculean exegetical efforts to analyze a text in its totality—treating its lexical, grammatical, semantic, syntactical, rhetorical, historical, cultural, theological, literary, ideological, and sociological dimensions, not to mention accounting for the complexities of reception and application—lead to piecemeal, *dis*-integrated treatments of particular passages.

Critics decontextualize the Petrine household code in a number of ways. One should already be obvious: they isolate it from the context of the rest of the epistle. Some scholars do so intentionally, arguing that the code is a later redactor's addition to Peter's original composition. It is more common for this decontextualization to occur implicitly through neglect of the code's resonances with other prominent Petrine language and themes. As discussed further below, exegetes also frequently break the code into smaller subunits and analyze them separately. A prominent example is the *hymnos*, or praise song, found in 1 Pet. 2:21–25:

> 21 For to this you have been called, because Christ also suffered for you, leaving you an example, so that you should follow in his steps.
> 22 "He committed no sin, and no deceit was found in his mouth."
> 23 When he was abused, he did not return abuse; when he suffered, he did not threaten; but he entrusted himself to the one who judges justly.
> 24 He himself bore our sins in his body on the cross, so that, free from sins, we might live for righteousness; by his wounds you have been healed.
> 25 For you were going astray like sheep, but now you have returned to the shepherd and guardian of your souls.

Scholars have devoted considerable time and energy to: 1) determining whether the letter writer composed this passage himself or incorporated it from elsewhere; 2) identifying its exact generic species (e.g., *encomium*, *epainos*, Christian liturgical prose, etc.); and 3) comparing the values espoused in the hymn, especially those evident in Christ's behavior, to those of the surrounding extratextual culture.

3.8   *Benefits of a Rhetorical Approach*

A rhetorical approach shifts our attention to the basic recognition that, whatever his source(s), Peter aims to influence by appealing to established cultural norms that he must assume his audience already considers authoritative. We should not overlook the fact that Peter takes the traditional organization of an *oikos* for granted, letting it stand undefended and unexplained; his focus is on using its categories to exemplify his larger rhetorical point: Christian submission to suffering is exemplary and thus serves an evangelistic purpose.

Certainly, Peter could have taken a different approach. The letter's appeal to suffering as exemplary evangelism presupposes that its addressees continue to live and suffer together amongst unbelievers, since Christians could not influence non-Christians in this way if they lived cloistered away from the broader society.[36] In contrast, Jewish apocalyptic texts from roughly the same time period, such as the sectarian literature of Qumran, advocate literal separation from unbelievers in response to suffering.[37] Peter does not recommend physical isolationism in the face of suffering. Instead, he envisions Christians following Christ's example of submitting to suffering while remaining *within* the established kyriarchical structures of the Roman Empire. One benefit of a rhetorical approach is that it helps us see how, even as 1 Peter's rhetoric creates boundaries around a beleaguered Christian community, those communal boundaries are relatively permeable.

Rhetoric also highlights how, regardless of Peter's intentions, his appeal to an already-authoritative household structure would have landed differently for different readers. Top of mind for some of the letter's recipients may have been past slave rebellions and uprisings, such as the relatively recent murder of

---

36   Twenty years ago, Balch critiqued Elliott for overstating points of coherence between Petrine and Qumranic communities, though scholars after Elliott have drawn similar connections. See, e.g., Schutter 1989: 192. Benjamin Sargent's monograph mentions that the Qumran community advocated "practical disengagement and withdrawal, *in contrast to* the communities represented by 1 Peter," but this recognition has little impact on his argument, which presupposes a sectarian apocalypticism *shared by* 1 Peter and the Qumran scrolls (Sargent: 2015: 149. Emphasis added).

37   Ancient apocalyptic literature reflects varying degrees of sectarianism, and often reflects a separatist self-consciousness even when specific references to sectarianism do not appear. See, among others, Collins 2014, 2009; for a different approach to similar questions, see Regev 2007.

Lucius Pedanius Secundus by one of those enslaved in his household in 61 CE, and the harsh retaliation exacted by the Roman Senate, which then ordered all those enslaved by Secundus to be executed regardless of their involvement in the murder (Tac., *Ann.* 14:42–45). Those readers likely would have heard Peter's instructions differently from readers whose interests were piqued by, say, the household code's contrast between internal and physical adornment, common in Hellenistic philosophical writings (3:3–4; see also 1 Tim. 2:9–10), or by the stories about Abraham and Sarah from Genesis (3:6), or by any of the other infinite factors that arrest attention and influence comprehension.

Another benefit of a rhetorical approach is that it can contribute to a more nuanced historical picture of the first century CE than the one we find in most twentieth-century biblical scholarship. Throughout the twentieth century, scholars debated the degree to which early Christians exhibited and/or interacted with Greco-Roman *as opposed to* Jewish cultural norms. In recent decades, historians have reconstructed a more nuanced cultural landscape, demonstrating that, in many ways, "Greco-Roman *versus* Jewish" is a misleading dichotomy. In general, first-century CE Jews were Hellenized, a minority people living in a culturally-dominant imperial world. At the same time, there were distinctives that made them Jewish, and even Hellenized Jews were not equally Hellenized or Hellenized in the same ways. Rhetoric helps us to move beyond such either/or formulations to recognize the great variability and unreliability of rhetorical strategies and effects. Peter's household code may have been differently (or not at all) persuasive to members of various people groups—Hellenized, Jewish, and otherwise.

To give a specific example, most critics agree that the so-called Christ hymn of 1 Peter 2:21–25 fits under the broad rhetorical category of *epideictic*, or praise language. Most also agree that when compared to standard Greco-Roman epideictic conventions, however, there is an oddity: the qualities and actions that Peter praises in Christ challenge, rather than reflect, classical rhetoricians' conceptions of praiseworthy qualities and actions. The first-century CE rhetorician Theon, for example, defines *enkōmion* as "language revealing the greatness of virtuous actions and other good qualities belonging to a particular person" (109). Theon specifically identifies as his example for emulation Alexander of Macedon, who "overthrew many great peoples" (110). Peter, in contrast, praises Christ not for overthrowing anyone, but for the exact opposite: although Christ had the power to "threaten" and "abuse," he chose instead to submit himself to suffering on behalf of others (2:23). Martin and Nash's description of the closest New Testament parallel to this passage, the encomiastic Pauline "Christ hymn" in Phil. 2:6–11, could just as well fit 1 Pet. 2:21–25:

> The *hymnos* genre is taken up in a manner that subverts Greco-Roman notions of honour and status and establishes for the Christian community new standards by which honour and status are to be ascribed. (2015: 93)

Praising Christ's example of submitting oneself willingly to suffering may have been unusual when compared with normative Greco-Roman notions of exemplarity as commensurate with honor and status. It aligns well, however, with the values espoused in other Jewish literature. As commentators routinely note, embedded within the Christ hymn of 1 Pet. 2, we find a citation from the book of Isaiah: "He committed no sin, and no deceit was found in his mouth" (1 Pet. 2:22; Isa. 53:9b). Some see the entire passage as Petrine commentary on the longstanding Jewish expectations for a Messiah who would come as a "Suffering Servant." Peter portrays Jesus as that long-awaited Messiah.

Comparing the Petrine Christ hymn to classical Greco-Roman rhetorical conventions on the one hand, and to Isaianic messianic expectations on the other, leads easily to the familiar dichotomy mentioned above: scholars treat the hymn as *either* "Jewish" *or* "Greco-Roman." A rhetorical approach allows for more expansive diversity amongst its readers. For instance, the citation of Second Isaiah in 1 Pet. 2:21–25 presents an instance of exemplarity shaped by intertextuality. Readers' responses inevitably will be shaped by their conceptions of that prior text or tradition. Most likely, Peter's portrayal of Christ's example as a willing and silent sufferer would be persuasive for those in his rhetorical audience who considered Isaiah 53 and/or the Suffering Servant tradition to be authoritative. Those who did not know that strand of Jewish discourse, or who admired Roman imperial dominance over submission, on the other hand, might find Christ's exemplarity in 1 Peter to be more confusing than compelling.

Attending to rhetoric can free us from habitual interpretive assumptions and widen the aperture of discussions regarding the household code in 1 Peter. As I noted above, some scholars think the presence of a household code in 1 Peter indicates a move *away* from apocalyptic expectations, but this is untenable if we treat the code as an integrated aspect of Peter's larger epistolary project. What if, instead of presuming that the Petrine *Haustafel* signals a shift *away* from apocalyptic thinking, we understood it in precisely the opposite way—i.e., not as an exception to Peter's Jewish apocalyptic discourse on suffering, but as a crucial component of it? What might change if we read the household code as an integrated and integral part of the letter's rhetorically-shaped response to its audience's perceived suffering, oriented around and motivated by an apocalyptic understanding of the world?

Recalling the results of the analysis above, 1 Peter, like other Jewish apocalyptic discourses, depicts suffering as: 1) temporary, eventually leading to eternal glory; 2) corporeal and likely severe for subordinated members of a hierarchy; 3) unjustly imposed by outsiders onto innocent insiders; and 4) its own form of exemplarity. Reading the household code within these broader discussions of suffering brings a new set of emphases into stark relief.

3.9 Reading the Household Code as Jewish Apocalyptic Rhetoric: An Appeal to Exemplarity in Response to Suffering

On the micro-level, two of the Petrine code's unique particularities come to the fore when we read the code within a Jewish apocalyptic framework.[38] The first is Peter's direction to husbands to live together with their wives *kata gnōsin*, "according to knowledge" (3:7). One characteristic of Jewish apocalyptic literature is its privileging of *gnōsis* ("knowledge," especially of an esoteric or mystical nature). As the etymology of "apocalypse" suggests (lit.: revealing, uncovering), one of the defining features of apocalyptic discourse is its concern with the revelation of secret or hidden knowledge. Yet, most English translations erase the phrase's resonance with this wider tradition. Though some English translations render the phrase literally, "according to knowledge" (KJV; RHE; WEB; YLT), it is more frequently translated with phrases such as "considerately" (RSV); "show consideration" (NRSV); "in an understanding way" (ESV; NAS; NCV); "be considerate" (NIV); "with understanding" (NKJV; NLT). Some connect *kata gnōsin* directly with the following clause, as though the knowledge to which Peter refers is clearly the wives' weakness: "live with your wives with a clear recognition of the fact that they are weaker than you" (WNT); "by knowing, give ye honour to the woman's frailty" (WYC); "live with your wives with the proper understanding that they are more delicate than you" (GNT).

It is entirely plausible, both grammatically and conceptually, that Peter's husbandly *gnōsis* refers not to the wife's weak nature, nor to a generally benevolent "considerate" attitude husbands should have toward their wives, but rather, to a broader understanding about the world—a privileged Christian *gnōsis*—that the letter itself aims to reveal and inculcate. The sense of the verse would then be something like: "Husbands, likewise, live together with [your wives] according to the *gnōsis* [that is revealed here] ..." The author of the Second Epistle of Peter uses the term in this way, calling his readers to

---

38   Peter's *Haustafel* is also unusual in that it diverges from the traditional pairings of husband-wife, father-child, master-slave, omitting any reference to parents or children. On "eight major ways in which the Petrine *Haustafel* deviates from the previous pattern [in Colossians]," see Bauman-Martin 2004: 263.

support their "goodness with *gnōsis*, and *gnōsis* with self-control" (1:5), and to "grow in the grace and *gnōsis* of our Lord and Savior Jesus Christ" (3:18).

Second, as David Horrell has argued, Peter's repeated references to the wives' "way of life" (*anastrophē*, mentioned twice in 3:1–2) cohere well with contemporaneous Jewish notions of group identity. This conception of what it means to be a people is not entirely based on shared blood or common origins; it is also forged through, and outwardly identifiable by, shared behaviors, or patterns of conduct (*anastrophē*). Peter speaks of Jesus followers rejecting the futile *anastrophē* they inherited from their ancestors (1:18) in favor of pursuing a "good *anastrophē* in Christ" (3:16)—an *anastrophē* that is marked by holiness and honor (1:15; 2:12). Horrell detects an "ethno-cultural" dimension to these uses of *anastrophē*, drawing parallels to Galatians 1:13 and 2 Maccabees 6:23, where *anastrophē* refers specifically to Judaism as a way of life.[39] In other Jewish literature, a similar sentiment appears even when the word *anastrophē* does not. Josephus, for example, offers "a gracious welcome" to proselytes, declaring that "it is not race alone which constitutes relationship but also the deliberate choice of a way of life (*tou biou*)" (*C. Ap.* 2.210). Challenging New Testament scholars' penchant for constructing "a dichotomy between an ethnically particular Judaism and a universal, open, trans-ethnic Christianity," Horrell reads Peter's instructions—including the mentions of wives' *anastrophē* in the household code (3:1–2)—as similar to the kind of group-identity formation in which Jewish writers of the time were engaged (Horrell 2016: 439).

These micro-level aspects of the text stand out when the household code is read as belonging to the epistle's Jewish apocalyptic rhetoric. On a macro-level, discourses of exemplarity can help us to understand how the code functions rhetorically within that context. For one thing, it sees submission within a brutal social system as a form of suffering. 1 Peter can be read as more than an exhortation to embrace cultural accommodation. The letter commends submission as a temporary trial in the face of an imminent eschaton—a temporary trial that has beneficial exemplary effects. Suffering—including submission within rigid social hierarchies—is bearable precisely because "the world as now constituted is not the end" (Collins 1998: 282). I do not mean to say that the writer of this first-century letter was a (proto-)feminist or democratic egalitarian who rejected hierarchy altogether. However, I do see Peter connecting Christ's exemplary suffering to submission within an oppressive kyriarchal social system. For Peter, Christ's suffering is not limited to the physical pain he endured on the cross. His submission is honored as a form of suffering, as

---

39   Recognizing that the term *anastrophē* has multiple meanings, Horrell observes that in the
      NT epistles, it consistently refers to "behavior, conduct or way of life" (Horrell 2016: 453).

well. By extension, the experiences of the subordinated members of household hierarchies are similarly held up as examples of endurance in suffering.

This suggests, moreover, that there is a sense in which all of Peter's instructions to specific subgroups within the *oikos* are paradigmatic for the whole community, regardless of station or rank. Interpreters often assume that the instructions in 2:18–25 are uniquely applicable to enslaved people, the directions in 3:1–6 are strictly meant for married women, and the exhortation in 3:7 applies only to married men.[40] However, a number of factors commend *not* reading Peter's sets of instructions as directly applicable *only* to particular subsets of people in his audience, but rather, reading them as rhetorically-crafted illustrative examples of the Christian "way of life" to which he calls all followers of Christ.

One such factor is that, in the Greek, Peter's instructions are both intricately interconnected to one another and subordinated to larger concerns, a fact that English translations and added subheadings generally conceal. The code begins with an overarching note about the importance of honorable conduct amongst Gentiles (2:11–12). Verse 13 then commands: "Accept the authority (*hupotassō*) of every human institution for the Lord's sake." Note that *hupotassō* is the only finite verb until the imperatives *timaō*, *agapaō*, and *phobeō* in 2:17: "Honor (*timaō*) all, love (*agapaō*) the brotherhood, fear (*phobeō*) God, honor (*timaō*) the king." Everything that follows *hupotassō* in 2:13–17 qualifies or explains what it means to accept the authority of human institutions "for the Lord's sake." Grammatically, the exhortations to enslaved people do not begin a separate statement. Instead, Peter uses the participial form of *hupotassō* in v. 18 ("slaves, accept*ing* the authority of your masters ..."). By using the participle, Peter presents enslaved people as one example of the more general commands to "honor all, love the brotherhood, fear God, and honor the king" in verse 17. When Peter shifts his address from slaves to wives in 3:1, he again uses the participial form of *hupotassō*, and adds the adverb *homoiōs* ("likewise" or "in the same way"): "wives, likewise, accept*ing* the authority of your own husbands ..." In this way, Peter grammatically connects the directives for wives to the admonitions that precede them for the enslaved. When he turns to address the husbands in 3:7, he employs new verbs (*sunoikeō*, "to live with," and *aponemō*, "to show"), but he again uses the participial forms and the adverb *homoiōs*, thereby wedding the guidelines for husbands to those for both wives and slaves ("husbands, likewise, liv*ing* with ... and show*ing* ...").

---

40   We have here another example of how a piecemeal approach effaces certain aspects of
        the Petrine *Haustafel*.

In other words, the verses from 2:18 to 3:7 constitute one connected unit of thought, all of which is subordinate to 2:17 ("honor all, love the brotherhood, fear God, and honor the king"), which is itself an elaboration of 2:13 ("accept the authority of every human institution for the Lord's sake"). Peter uses the categories of enslaved people, wives, and husbands as concrete examples to illustrate his broader instructions. What's more, these instructions are not applicable *only* within the traditional Roman *oikos*. Peter ties the list of household examples to what follows with the phrase *to de telos*, "and finally" (3:8), and a direct address drawing all recipients together with adjectives emphasizing unity: "all who are of one mind" (*pantes homophrones*), "having shared-feeling" (*sumpatheis*), those who "share brotherly love" (*philadelphoi*), are "compassionate" (*eusplagchnoi*), "have humble minds" (*tapeinophrones*), and so on. Instead of treating Peter's instructions as isolated bits of advice that are solely applicable to separate people groups, we might see them functioning together like carefully-placed dominoes, falling one into another toward the same ultimate persuasive end.

The order of these interconnected examples is not insignificant. The substructure of Peter's argument mirrors the first-century hierarchy to which he refers, but he addresses each category in reverse order: beginning at the bottom, he addresses enslaved people (perceived as inferior to both wives and husbands), then wives (superior to those enslaved, but inferior to husbands), then husbands (superior to both prior categories). The form, then, reflects the counter-cultural principles to which it speaks. By addressing enslaved people first, Peter effectively renders their example "paradigmatic for all the recipients of the letter," not only for those who are themselves literally enslaved (Moxnes 2014: 138–39).

The wives, similarly, can be read as exemplary models for the entire Petrine community. As Horrell underscores, Jewish notions of the "way of life" (*anastrophē*) to which Peter refers in 3:1–2 are hardly applicable only to wives or to women. Indeed, "the pattern of conduct here demanded of wives [in 3:1–6] is to a considerable degree demanded also of the whole community in 3.13–17" (Horrell 2016: 455). Peter's trust in the persuasive power of exemplary conduct is further evident in his use of the word *apeithousin* (which derives from *apeithō*, "to be unpersuaded") to describe non-Christian husbands in verse 1: "wives, likewise, accepting the authority of your own husbands, so that even if some are not persuaded (*apeithousin*) by the word, they might be won over by their wives' *anastrophē*." The wives are thus held up as exemplars of the evangelistically effective exemplarity commended elsewhere in the epistle.

Reading the household code through the lens of exemplarity in a context of Jewish apocalyptic suffering also sheds new light on the intriguing reference to

Sarah in 1 Pet. 3:6. Peter's use of the Jewish matriarch has long been a *crux inter-pretum* in New Testament studies. Clearly, Peter makes an example of Sarah. But while all agree that she is presented as a positive exemplar, the nature of her exemplarity and how it functions rhetorically in a context of apocalyptic suffering are ambiguous. Is Sarah's example the same as or different from Christ's example of suffering? Does the call to imitate her represent an exemplary but ultimately unattainable goal, like Peter's injunction to imitate God earlier in the letter ("As he who called you is holy, be holy yourselves in all your conduct; for it is written, 'You shall be holy, for I am holy,'" 1:15–16), or is Sarah presented as an ideal that readers can and should reach and replicate?

Scholars have mainly sought to determine the sense in which Sarah "called Abraham lord" by pinpointing an exact source text(s) to which 1 Peter alludes.[41] Still, the text to which Peter refers remains disputed, since Sarah only literally calls Abraham "lord" (*kyrios*) once, in Gen. 18:12 (LXX), and she does not do so there in a context of obedience; other popular proposals for source texts include Gen. 12:11–20 and 20:1–18, where Sarah does obey Abraham, but does not actually refer to him as *kyrios*.[42] Sarah's relationship with Abraham, and her harsh treatment of the enslaved Egyptian Hagar, make her a complicated choice as an exemplar of holy women. Schneider declares that Peter "sanitizes" Sarah (Schneider 2004: 132), while Sly argues that Peter intentionally reshapes her into "the image of the ideal Hellenistic wife" because "some details in the Genesis account of Sarah and Abraham's marriage were embarrassing to men in the Hellenistic age" (Sly 1991: 126, 129). While these represent valuable research questions, they do not chiefly concern the persuasive functions of Sarah's multilayered exemplarity within the context of 1 Peter's overall rhetorical message.

I contend that the paradoxes and ambiguities of exemplarity generate Sarah's rhetorical power. As we saw with Peter's use of Christ's example, Sarah simultaneously stands apart as a conspicuous example of holiness *and* typifies a model of suffering submission that can and should be copied. Adapting Derrida's observation that exemplarity "inscribes the universal in the proper body of a singularity, of an idiom or culture," Sarah inscribes the universal in the proper body of 1 Peter's singularity (Derrida 1992: 72). Situated at the interstices between universality and particularity, between the authority of the past and Peter's vision for the future, Sarah represents "a kind of textual

---

41   Debates also continue about the implications of this reference for gender relations today. The two extremes are that 1 Pet. 3:5–6 indicates that every wife universally should submit to her husband "as she submits to the Lord" (e.g., Knight 1991: 174), or it reinforces a patriarchical phallocentrism that ought to be rejected today (e.g., Schüssler Fiorenza 1992: 4).

42   On other possible sources, and the relevance of original context for early Jewish and Christian interpretation (or lack thereof), see Bar-Asher Siegal and Dinkler 2020.

node or point of juncture," at which hermeneutical processes and rhetorical desires come together to transform an honored figure from the Jewish past into a source of inspiration for Christian transformation in the present. In my view, Peter's employment of Sarah therefore functions much like the discourses of Roman exemplarity discussed above; replicating Sarah's exemplarity becomes, for Peter, a Christian form of "social reproduction."

The second part of the reference to Sarah deepens these resonances. Peter declares that imitating Sarah results in fruitful multiplication (i.e., more copies of her): "You have become her children (*tekna*) as long as you *keep doing* what is good (*agathopoiousai*, a present active conditional participle) and never let fears alarm you" (3:6). Interpreters have understood this metaphor in various ways, but few have noticed the rhetorical role of exemplarity therein. Referring to Sarah as a reproducing mother implicitly reinforces the explicit claims elsewhere in 1 Peter that exemplary suffering can lead to conversion and thereby increase the numbers of Christian believers. Moreover, this call to emulation and replication is not limited to females. Although many translations read, "You have become her daughters" (YLT; WYC; TYN, NRS; NLT; KJV; NIV; GNT), Peter uses the generic term *tekna*, "children," *not* the gender-specific *thugateres*, "daughters," indicating that anyone who continually does what is good and remains unafraid can become Sarah's *tekna*, or heirs (Horrell 2016: 455).

To sum up this final section, I have argued that the Petrine *Haustafel* is not an exception to the Jewish apocalyptic discourse of the letter as a whole. Instead of decontextualizing the household code or treating subsections of it separately, we ought to read it as an intricately interconnected unit of examples, presented to support Peter's larger persuasive aims. One of those aims is to address the perceived exigence of Christian suffering at the hands of non-Christians. Throughout the epistle, Peter commends submission to suffering as a form of exemplarity that is both community-building for Christians and beneficial for those who might convert as a result of witnessing this "way of life." Tying the tightly woven threads of 1 Pet. 2:13–3:7 in with the rhetorical discourses of suffering and exemplarity at work throughout the letter illuminates how the household code presents both named individuals and broader social categories as paradigmatic and hopefully persuasive examples of Peter's more general claims.

Conclusion

This volume began by invoking the astronauts' breathtaking space-station snapshots of the Grand Canyon, photographs that encapsulate in one frozen frame the effects of millennia. One click of a shutter rendered the Colorado River's majestic movement both static and timeless. In still images, the river's rushing immensity, its power to cut deep and wide into the Earth, appear to be given, as though the resulting Canyon simply and inevitably *is*.

Considering the breadth and depth of the Bible's influence from the shutter-click of now can give the same impression: captured by its long-revered canonicity, the majesty of the Bible's movements appears fixed, absolute, as though its power to shape humanity's landscape simply *is*. With this volume, I have sought to persuade you otherwise. My goal has been to convince you, my readers, that the Bible's influence is—and has always been—fluid and changing, the result of an "unending conversation" that is always "still vigorously in progress" (Burke 1941: 11); that biblical texts are by nature rhetorical; and that, consequently, biblical interpreters ought to be thinking carefully and intentionally about both the rhetoric of biblical texts *and* the rhetoric we use when we interpret them.

Heeding Bizzell and Herzberg's advice to "look at the many definitions [rhetoric] has accumulated over the years and to attempt to understand how each arose and how each still inhabits and shapes the field" of rhetorical studies, the first major section traced how rhetoric has been studied in two very different time periods: the classical period of Greco-Roman antiquity, and the modern period of the twentieth and twenty-first centuries (Bizzell and Herzberg 2001: 1). I then introduced how various understandings of rhetoric arose in and shaped the subfields of Hebrew Bible and New Testament studies. The final section analyzed the Jewish apocalyptic rhetoric of the First Epistle of Peter, focusing especially on how the letter advances the view that suffering is an influential form of exemplarity. Overall, I hope to have given readers a glimpse of how the resources of rhetorical studies can help us to understand the many and varied ways that humans pick up and wield biblical texts in our efforts to influence the people and the world around us.

I shall conclude by echoing Booth, who closes his metacritical manifesto, *The Rhetoric of Rhetoric*, with characteristic urgency:

> Whether you are inside the academy or outside, doing politics or business, practicing philanthropy or chicanery, now is the time to start studying critically the floods of good rhetoric and rhetrickery that sweep over you daily.
>
> BOOTH 2004: 172

Floods of good rhetoric and rhetrickery sweep over us daily, in-fluencing the directions of biblical scholarship, the beliefs and behaviors of churches and societies, the tenor and trajectories of our public and private conversations.

It is crucial, then, to know how to think critically about rhetoric and biblical interpretation.

Now is the time to start studying.

Acknowledgments

I am writing this in the fall of 2020, as the COVID pandemic and its attendant ills continue to disrupt life on a global scale. Like so many last spring, my daily work unexpectedly shifted to a job for which I am woefully untrained (home-schooling my children), and my partner's work as a physician took on newly weighty dimensions of risk and consequence. In such a world, completing a manuscript about biblical interpretation initially struck me as both pointless and impossible. Yet, for reasons that should become clear as this book unfolds, it is precisely in such a world—when collective trauma and chaos are calling us to do and be better together—that sustained attention to biblical interpretation becomes both imperative and urgent.

And so it is that in the midst of this blessed unrest, my debts and gratitude run even deeper than they did before. I am grateful to Dean Gregory Sterling and my colleagues at Yale Divinity School, especially Yii-Jan Lin and Laura Nasrallah, for their support, and to Yale University for the research leave that made it possible for me to complete the manuscript. Irene Peirano's expertise in ancient rhetoric enhanced my grasp of the complexities of these ancient discussions; co-teaching with Irene was a delight, not least because of the diverse intellectual enthusiasms of the students in our graduate seminar, "Rhetorics of the Ancient World." I am thankful to Scott Elliott for his invaluable feedback on this volume, and for continuing a conversation first sparked at an Annual Meeting of the Society of Biblical Literature years ago. Thanks to Michal Bar-Asher Siegal, whose interest in a draft of Part 3 blossomed into an entirely separate co-written project, which we presented in Jerusalem, Israel, in March, 2019 (now in *Ephemerides Theologicae Lovanienses*, "Citing Sarah in the New Testament and Rabbinic Literature: Does Original Context Matter?").

Sections of this manuscript appear in earlier forms in "Between Intention and Reception: Textual Meaning-Making in Intersubjective Perspective," *Exegesis without Authorial Intention? Approaches to Textual Meaning* (Leiden: Brill, 2019), 72–93; "Rhetorical Narratology," *Oxford Handbook of New Testament Rhetoric* (Oxford: Oxford University Press, forthcoming); "New Testament Rhetorical Narratology: An Invitation toward Integration," *Biblical Interpretation* 24: 203–28. I appreciate the suggestions from reviewers and editors of those publications, which helped me improve what you will read here.

Sincere thanks to Tat-Siong Benny Liew, who invited me to contribute to the series, to Davina Lopez, who encouraged me to complete the manuscript, to Brill's anonymous reviewers for supporting its publication, and to Matt Klem for his expert copy-editing skills.

My most abiding gratitude goes to John, Alethea, and Daelen, who cheered me on as I wrangled ideas and set words to page, and who brought me coffee in the wee morning hours before each day living and learning in quarantine began in earnest.

Works Cited

Achtemeier, Paul J. 1996. *1 Peter* (Hermeneia; Minneapolis: Fortress).

Alter, Robert. 1981. *The Art of Biblical Narrative* (New York: Basic Books).

Alter, Robert. 1985. *The Art of Biblical Poetry* (New York: Basic Books).

Anderson, Janice Capel. 1992. "Feminist Criticism: The Dancing Daughter," in Anderson and Moore (eds.): 111–43.

Anderson, Janice Capel and Stephen D. Moore. 2008. "Introduction: The Lives of Mark," in Anderson and Moore (eds.): 1–27.

Anderson, Janice Capel and Stephen D. Moore (eds.). 2008. *Mark & Method: New Approaches in Biblical Studies* (Minneapolis: Fortress, 2nd ed.).

Andrews, J. R. 1983. *The Practice of Rhetorical Criticism* (New York: Macmillan).

Ankersmit, Frank. 1989. *The Reality Effect in the Writing of History: The Dynamics of Historiographical Topology* (Amsterdam: Noord-Hollandsche).

Arendt, Hannah. 1958. *The Human Condition* (Chicago: University of Chicago Press).

Attridge, Harold W. 2013. "The Samaritan Woman: A Woman Transformed," in Steven A. Hunt, D. François Tolmie, and Ruben Zimmermann (eds.), *Character Studies in the Fourth Gospel: Narrative Approaches to Seventy Figures in John* (Tübingen: Mohr Siebeck): 268–81.

Auerbach, Erich. 1957. *Mimesis: The Representation of Reality in Western Literature* (Princeton: Princeton University Press).

Aune, David E. 1981. "Review of H. D. Betz, *Galatians: A Commentary on Paul's Letter to the Churches of Galatia*," *RelSRev* 7: 323–28.

Bal, Mieke. 2002. *Travelling Concepts in the Humanities: A Rough Guide* (Toronto: University of Toronto Press).

Balch, David L. 1981. *Let Wives Be Submissive: The Domestic Code in 1 Peter* (Atlanta: SBL).

Balch, David L. 1986. "Hellenization/Acculturation in I Peter," in Charles H. Talbert (ed.), *Perspectives on First Peter* (Macon: Mercer University Press): 79–101.

Bar-Asher Siegal, Michal and Michal Beth Dinkler. 2020. "Citing Sarah in the New Testament and Rabbinic Literature: Does Original Context Matter?," *Ephemerides Theologicae Lovanienses* 96: 443–57.

Barthes, Roland. 1968. "L'Effet de Réel," *Communications* 11: 84–89.

Barthes, Roland. 1974. *S/Z: An Essay* (trans. Richard Miller; New York: Hill & Wang).

Baumann-Martin, Betsy. 2004. "Women on the Edge: New Perspectives on Women in the Petrine Haustafel," *JBL* 123: 253–79.

Beasley-Murray, George. 1987. *John* (WBC 36; Waco, TX: Word).

Bechtler, Steven Richard. 1998. *Following in His Steps: Suffering, Community, and Christology in 1 Peter* (Atlanta: Scholars).

Bender, John B. and David E. Wellbery. 1990. *The Ends of Rhetoric: History, Theory, Practice* (Stanford, CA: Stanford University Press).

Benoit, William. 1980. "Aristotle's Example: The Rhetorical Induction," *Quarterly Journal of Speech* 66: 182–92.

Benoit, William. 1987. "On Aristotle's Example," *Philosophy and Rhetoric* 20: 261–67.

Berlin, Adele. 1985. *The Dynamics of Biblical Parallelism* (Bloomington: Indiana University Press).

Betz, Hans Dieter. 1975. "Literary Composition and Function of Paul's Letter to the Galatians," *NTS* 21: 353–79.

Betz, Hans Dieter. 1979. *Galatians: A Commentary on Paul's Letter to the Churches in Galatia* (Hermeneia; Philadelphia: Fortress).

Betz, Hans Dieter. 1985. *Second Corinthians 8 and 9: A Commentary on Two Administrative Letters of the Apostle Paul* (Hermeneia; Philadelphia: Fortress).

Betz, Hans Dieter. 1995. *The Sermon on the Mount: A Commentary on the Sermon on the Mount, including the Sermon on the Plain (Matthew 5:3–7:27 and Luke 6:20–49)* (Hermeneia; Minneapolis: Fortress).

Bird, Jennifer G. 2013. *Abuse, Power and Fearful Obedience: Reconsidering 1 Peter's Commands to Wives* (London: Bloomsbury).

Bitzer, Lloyd. 1968. "The Rhetorical Situation," *Philosophy and Rhetoric* 1: 1–14.

Bizzell, Patricia and Bruce Herzberg (eds.). 2001. *The Rhetorical Tradition: Readings from Classical Times to the Present* (Boston: Bedford/St. Martin's).

Black, Clifton. 2001. *The Rhetoric of the Gospel: Theological Artistry in the Gospels and Acts* (Louisville, KY: Westminster John Knox).

Boismard, M.-E. 1973. "Aenon, Près de Salem," *Revue Biblique* 80: 223–26.

Bonner, Stanley. 1977. *Education in Ancient Rome: From the Elder Cato to the Younger Pliny* (Berkeley: University of California Press).

Booth, Wayne C. 1974. *Modern Dogma and the Rhetoric of Assent* (Chicago: University of Chicago Press).

Booth, Wayne C. 2004. *The Rhetoric of Rhetoric: The Quest for Effective Communication* (Malden: Blackwell).

Borchert, Gerald. 1982. "The Conduct of Christians in the Face of the 'Fiery Ordeal' (1 Pet 4:12–5:11)," *Review & Expositor* 79: 451–62.

Botha, Jan. 1989. "On the 'Reinvention' of Rhetoric," *Scriptura* 31: 14–31.

Botha, J. Eugene. 1990. "Reader 'Entrapment' and Literary Device in John 4:1–42," *Neot* 24: 37–47.

Botha, J. Eugene. 1991. *Jesus and the Samaritan Woman: A Speech Act Reading of John 4:1–42* (Leiden: Brill).

Bovon, François. 1978. "Foi chrétienne et religion populaire dans la première Epître de Pierre," *ETR* 53: 25–41.

Boyarin, Daniel. 1995. "Take the Bible for Example: Midrash as Literary Theory," in Alexander Gelley (ed.), *Unruly Examples: On the Rhetoric of Exemplarity* (Stanford, CA: Stanford University Press): 27–47.

Brown, Raymond E. *The Gospel according to John (i–xii)* (AB 29; New York: Doubleday).

Brueggemann, Walter. 1997. *Theology of the Old Testament: Testimony, Dispute, Advocacy* (Minneapolis: Fortress).

Bryant, Donald C. 1965. "Rhetoric: Its Function and Scope," *Quarterly Journal of Speech* 39: 401–24.

Buell, Denise Kimber. 2005. *Why This New Race? Ethnic Reasoning in Early Christianity* (New York: Columbia University Press).

Burke, Kenneth. 1931. *Counter-Statement* (Berkeley: University of California Press).

Burke, Kenneth. 1941. *The Philosophy of Literary Form* (Berkeley: University of California Press).

Burke, Kenneth. 1953. *A Grammar of Motives* (New York: Prentice Hall).

Burke, Kenneth. 1969. *A Rhetoric of Motives* (Berkeley: University of California Press).

Burton, Vicki Tolar. 1999. "The Speaker Respoken: Material Rhetoric as Feminist Methodology," *College English* 61: 545–73.

Buxton, Richard. 1982. *Persuasion in Greek Tragedy: A Study of Peitho* (Cambridge: Cambridge University Press).

Calfhill, James. 1565. *An Answere to the Treatise of the Cross* (London: Denham).

Campbell, Barth L. 1998. *Honor, Shame, and the Rhetoric of 1 Peter* (Atlanta: Scholars).

Capes, David B. 2003. "Imitatio Christi and the Gospel Genre." *BBR*: 1–19.

Carey, Greg. 2005. *Ultimate Things: An Introduction to Jewish and Christian Apocalyptic Literature* (St. Louis: Chalice).

Carey, Greg and L. Gregory Bloomquist (eds.) 1999. *Vision and Persuasion: Rhetorical Dimensions of Apocalyptic Discourse* (St. Louis: Chalice).

Carter, Warren. 2004. "Going All the Way? Honoring the Emperor and Sacrificing Wives and Slaves in 1 Peter 2.13–3.6," in A. J. Levine (ed.), *A Feminist Companion to the Catholic Epistles and Hebrews* (London: T&T Clark): 14–33.

Charney, Davida. 2015. *Persuading God: Rhetorical Studies of First-Person Psalms* (Sheffield: Sheffield-Phoenix).

Chin, M. 1991. "A Heavenly Home for the Homeless: Aliens and Strangers in 1 Peter," *TynB* 42: 96–112.

Clark, Donald Lehman. 1957. *Rhetoric in Greco-Roman Education* (New York: Columbia University Press).

Clark, Elizabeth. 2004. *History, Theory, Text: Historians and the Linguistic Turn* (Cambridge, MA: Harvard University Press).

Classen, Carl Joachim. 1991. "Paulus und die antike Rhetorik," *ZNW* 82: 15–27.

Clines, David. 1996. *The Theme of the Pentateuch* (Sheffield: Sheffield Academic, 2nd ed.).

Collins, Adela Yarbro. 1984. *Crisis and Catharsis: The Power of the Apocalypse* (Philadelphia: Westminster/John Knox).

Collins, Adela Yarbro. 1986. "Introduction: Early Christian Apocalypticism," *Semeia* 36: 1–11.

Collins, John J. 1979. "Apocalypse: The Morphology of a Genre," *Semeia* 14: 1–20.

Collins, John J. 1998. *The Apocalyptic Imagination: An Introduction to Jewish Apocalyptic Literature* (Grand Rapids: Eerdmans, 2nd ed.).

Collins, John J. 2000. "From Prophecy to Apocalypticism: The Expectation of the End," in idem. (ed.), *The Encyclopedia of Apocalypticism, Vol. 1* (New York: Continuum): 129–61.

Collins, John J. 2009. *Beyond the Qumran Community: The Sectarian Movement of the Dead Sea Scrolls* (Grand Rapids: Eerdmans).

Collins, John J. 2014. *Scriptures and Sectarianism: Essays on the Dead Sea Scrolls* (WUNT 332; Tübingen: Mohr Siebeck).

Cook, Ryan. 2015. "Prayers That Form Us: Rhetoric and Psalms Interpretation," *JSOT* 39: 451–67.

Cook, Stephen. 1995. *Prophecy and Apocalypticism: The Post-exilic Social Setting* (Minneapolis: Fortress).

Corley, Kathleen. 1994. "1 Peter," in Elisabeth Schüssler Fiorenza (ed.), *Searching the Scriptures: A Feminist Commentary* (New York: Crossroad): 349–60.

Cribiore, Raffaela. 2001. *Gymnastics of the Mind: Greek Education in Hellenistic and Roman Egypt* (Princeton: Princeton University Press).

Crouch, James E. 1972. *The Origin and Intention of the Colossian Haustafel* (Göttingen: Vandenhoeck & Ruprecht).

Culpepper, Alan. 1987. *Anatomy of the Fourth Gospel: A Study in Literary Design* (Philadelphia: Fortress, 2nd ed.).

Darr, John. 1992. *On Character Building: The Reader and the Rhetoric of Characterization in Luke-Acts* (Louisville: Westminster/John Knox).

Darr, John. 1994. "'Watch How You Listen' (Lk. 8.18): Jesus and the Rhetoric of Perception in Luke-Acts," in E. S. Malbon and E. V. McKnight (eds.), *The New Literary Criticism and the New Testament* (Valley Forge, PA: Trinity Press International): 87–107.

DeLuca, Kevin M. 1999. *Image Politics: The New Rhetoric of Environmental Activism* (New York: Guilford Press).

Derrida, Jacques. 1992. *The Other Heading: Reflections on Today's Europe* (Bloomington: Indiana University Press).

deSilva, David. 2008. "Seeing Things John's Way: Rhetography and Conceptual Blending in Revelation 14:6–13," *BBR* 18: 271–98.

Dibelius, Martin. 1913. *An die Kolosser, Epheser, an Philemon* (HNT 12; Tübingen: Mohr [Siebeck]).

Dibelius, Martin. 1919. *Die Formgeschichte des Evangeliums* (Tübingen: Mohr [Siebeck]).

Dibelius, Martin. 1926. *Geschichte der urchristlicher Literatur 2* (Berlin: de Gruyter).

Dillon, John M. 1997. "The Pleasures and Perils of Soul-Gardening," in D. T. Runia and G. E. Sterling (eds.), *Studia Philonica Annual, Volume IX: Wisdom and Logos: Studies in Jewish Thought in Honor of David Winston* (Atlanta: Scholars): 190–97.

Dinkler, Michal Beth. 2016. "New Testament Rhetorical Narratology: An Invitation toward Integration." *Biblical Interpretation* 24: 203–28.

Dinkler, Michal Beth. 2019. "Between Intention and Reception: Textual Meaning-Making in Intersubjective Perspective," in Clarissa Breu (ed.), *Exegesis without Authorial Intention? Approaches to Textual Meaning* (Leiden: Brill): 72–93.

Dinkler, Michal Beth. Forthcoming. "Rhetorical Narratology," *Oxford Handbook of New Testament Rhetoric* (Oxford: Oxford University Press).

Dobbs-Allsopp, F. W. 2015. *On Biblical Poetry* (Oxford: Oxford University Press).

Douglass, Frederick. 1845. *Narrative of the Life of Frederick Douglass, An American Slave, Written by Himself* (Boston: The Anti-Slavery Office, No. 25 Cornhill).

Dozeman, Thomas B. 1992. "OT Rhetorical Criticism," in David Noel Freedman (ed.), *Anchor Bible Dictionary* (6 vols.; New York: Doubleday): 5:712–15.

Dryden, J. D. 2006. *Theology and Ethics in 1 Peter: Paraenetic Strategies for Christian Character Formation* (Tübingen: Mohr Siebeck).

Dubis, Mark. 2002. *Messianic Woes in First Peter: Suffering and Eschatology in 1 Peter 4: 12–19* (New York: Peter Lang).

duBois, Paige. 1995. *Sappho Is Burning* (Chicago: University of Chicago Press).

Dunning, Benjamin H. 2008. *Aliens and Sojourners: Self as Other in Early Christianity* (Divinations: Rereading Late Ancient Religion; Philadelphia: University of Pennsylvania Press).

Eagleton, Terry. 1983. *Literary Theory: An Introduction* (Oxford: Basil Blackwell).

Eagleton, Terry. 1991. *Ideology: An Introduction* (London: Verso).

Eisenbaum, Pamela M. 1997. *The Jewish Heroes of Christian History: Hebrews 11 in Literary Context* (Atlanta: Scholars).

Elliott, John H. 1981. *A Home for the Homeless: A Sociological Exegesis of 1 Peter, Its Situation and Strategy* (Philadelphia: Fortress).

Elliott, John H. 1986. "1 Peter, Its Situation and Strategy: A Discussion with David Balch," in Charles H. Talbert (ed.), *Perspectives on 1 Peter* (Macon, GA: Mercer University Press): 61–78.

Elliott, John H. 2000. *1 Peter* (AB 37; New York: Doubleday).

Elliott, John H. 2007. *Conflict, Community, and Honor: 1 Peter in Social Scientific Perspective* (Eugene, OR: Cascade).

Enenkel, Karl. 2001. "Strange and Bewildering Antiquity: Lipsius's Dialogue *Saturnales sermones* on Gladiatorial Games (1582)," in Karl Enenknel, Jan L. De Jong, and Jeanine De Landtsheer, with colloboration of Alicia Montoya (eds.) *Recreating Ancient History: Episodes from the Greek and Roman Past in the Arts and Literature of the Early Modern Period* (Leiden: Brill): 75–99.

Eslinger, Lyle. 1987. "The Wooing of the Woman at the Well: Jesus, the Reader, and Reader Response Criticism," *The Journal of Literature & Theology* 1: 167–83.

Feldmeier, Reinhard. 1992. *Die Christen als Fremde: Die Metaphor der Fremde in der antiken Welt, im Urchristentum und im 1. Petrusbrief* (Tübingen: Mohr Siebeck).

Fewell, Danna Nolan. 2016. "The Work of Biblical Narrative," in Danna Nolan Fewell (ed.), *The Oxford Handbook of Biblical Narrative* (Oxford: Oxford University Press): 3–26.

Fisher, Walter. 1986. "Judging the Quality of Audiences and Narrative Rationality," in J. L. Golden and J. J. Pilotta (eds.), *Practical Reasoning in Human Affairs* (D. Reidel Publishing): 85–103.

Fisk, Wilbur. 1831. "A Discourse on Predestination and Election: Preached on an Especial Occasion at Greenwich, Massachusetts" (Springfield, MA: Merriam, Little, & Co).

Flannery, Frances. 2014. "Dreams and Visions in Early Jewish and Early Christian Apocalypses and Apocalypticism," in John J. Collins (ed.), *The Oxford Handbook of Apocalyptic Literature* (Oxford: Oxford University Press): 104–20.

Flaschenriem, Barbara L. 2005. "Sulpicia and the Rhetoric of Disclosure," in Ellen Greene (ed.), *Women Poets in Ancient Greece and Rome* (Norman: University of Oklahoma Press): 169–91.

Foster, Robert and David Howard (eds.) 2008. *My Words Are Lovely: Studies in the Rhetoric of the Psalms* (LHBOTS 467; New York: T&T Clark).

Foucault, Michel. 1978. *The History of Sexuality. Vol. 1, An Introduction* (trans. Robert Hurley; New York: Vintage Books).

Foucault, Michel. 1988. *Technologies of the Self: A Seminar with Michel Foucault* (ed. L. H. Martin et al.; Amherst: University of Massachusetts Press).

Fowler, Robert M. 1991. *Let the Reader Understand: Reader-Response Criticism and the Gospel of Mark* (Minneapolis: Fortress).

Freedman, David Noel. 1986. "Deliberate Deviation from an Established Pattern of Repetition in Hebrew Poetry as a Rhetorical Device," in R. Giveon, M. Anbar, et. al. (eds.), *Proceedings of the Ninth World Congress of Jewish Studies, Division A: The Period of the Bible* (Jerusalem: Magnes): 45–52.

Fuchs, Esther. 1985. "The Literary Characterization of Mothers and Sexual Politics in the Hebrew Bible," in Adela Yarbro Collins (ed.), *Feminist Perspectives on Biblical Scholarship* (Chico: Scholars): 117–36.

Fuchs, Esther. 1993. "Structure, Ideology and Politics in the Biblical Betrothal Type-Scene," in Athalya Brenner (ed.), *Feminist Companion to Genesis* (Sheffield: Sheffield Academic): 273–81.

Fuchs, Esther. 2003. "Men in Biblical Feminist Scholarship," *JFSR* 19: 93–114.

Funk, Robert. 1966. *Language, Hermeneutic and Word of God* (New York: Harper & Row).

Funk, Robert, Roy Hoover, and the Jesus Seminar. 1993. *The Five Gospels: The Search for the Authentic Words of Jesus* (New York: The Macmillan Co.).

Gelley, Alexander (ed.). 1995. *Unruly Examples: On the Rhetoric of Exemplarity* (Stanford, CA: Stanford University Press).

Genette, Gérard. 1982. "Rhetoric Restrained," in Gérard Genette, *Figures of Literary Discourse* (trans. Alan Sheridan; Oxford: Blackwell): 103–26.

Gitay, Yehoshua. 1981. *Prophecy and Persuasion* (Bonn: Linguistica Biblica).

Gitay, Yehoshua. 1999. "Rhetorical Criticism," in McKenzie and Haynes (eds.): 135–49.

Gitay, Yehoshua. 2001. "Prophetic Criticism—'What Are They Doing?' The Case of Isaiah—A Methodological Assessment," *JSOT* 96: 101–27.

Glenn, Cheryl. 1997. *Rhetoric Retold: Regendering the Tradition from Antiquity through the Renaissance* (Carbondale: Southern Illinois University Press).

Goldhill, Simon. 2017. "The Limits of the Case Study: Exemplarity and the Reception of Classical Literature," *New Literary History* 48: 415–16.

Goppelt, Leonhard. 1978. *Der erste Petrusbrief* (ed. F. Hahn; Göttingen: Vandenhoeck und Ruprecht).

Grabbe, Lester (ed.). 2001. *Did Moses Speak Attic? Jewish Historiography and Scripture in the Hellenistic Period* (London: Bloomsbury).

Greenblatt, Stephen and Giles Gunn. 1992. "Introduction," in Stephen Greenblatt and Giles Gunn (eds.), *Redrawing the Boundaries: The Transformation of English and American Literary Studies* (New York: Modern Language Association of America): 1–11.

Grosz, Elizabeth. 1994. *Volatile Bodies. Towards a Corporeal Feminism* (Bloomington: Indiana University Press).

Hadot, Ilsetraut. 1969. *Seneca Und Die Griechisch-Römische Tradition Der Seelenleitung, Quellen Und Studien Zur Geschichte Der Philosophie* (Berlin: de Gruyter).

Hampton, Timothy. 1990. *Writing from History: The Rhetoric of Exemplarity in Renaissance Literature* (New York: Cornell University Press).

Harris, Randy. 2013. "The Rhetoric of Science Meets the Science of Rhetoric," *Poroi* 9: 1–12.

Haskins, Ekaterina. 2004. *Logos and Power in Isocrates and Aristotle* (Columbia, SC: University of South Carolina).

Hau, Lisa. 2016. *Moral History from Herodotus to Diodorus Siculus* (Edinburgh: Edinburgh University Press).

Hauser, Alan J. 1994. "Notes on History and Method," in Watson and Hauser: 3–20.

Hays, Richard. 1989. "'The Righteous One' as Eschatological Deliverer," in Joel Marcus and Marion Soards (eds.), *Apocalyptic and the New Testament: Essays in Honor of J. Louis Martyn* (Sheffield: Sheffield Academic): 191–215.

Hellholm, David. 1986. "The Problem of the Apocalyptic Genre and the Apocalypse of John," *Semeia* 36: 13–64.

Hesk, Jon. 1999. "The Rhetoric of Anti-Rhetoric in Athenian Oratory," in Simon Goldhill and Robin Osborne (eds.), *Performance Culture and Athenian Democracy* (Cambridge: Cambridge University Press): 201–30.

Hester, James D. 2010. "Rhetorics in and for the New Millennium," in James D. Hester and J. David Hester (eds.), *Rhetorics in the New Millennium: Promise and Fulfillment* (London: Bloomsbury): 1–20.

Hester Amador, J. D. 1999. *Academic Constraints in Rhetorical Criticism of the New Testament: An Introduction to a Rhetoric of Power* (Sheffield: Sheffield Academic).

Hill, David J. 1877. *The Science of Rhetoric: An Introduction to the Laws of Effective Discourse* (New York: Sheldon & Co.).

Himes, Paul. 2014. *Foreknowledge and Social Identity in 1 Peter* (Eugene, OR: Pickwick).

Hirsch, E. D. 1967. *Validity in Interpretation* (New Haven, CT: Yale University Press).

Hockey, Katherine M. 2019. *The Role of Emotion in 1 Peter* (Cambridge: Cambridge University Press).

Holdsworth, John. 1980. "The Sufferings in 1 Peter and 'Missionary Apocalyptic,'" in E. A. Livingstone (ed.), *Studia Biblica III* (JSNTSup 3; Sheffield: JSOT Press): 225–32.

Holloway, Paul. 2009. *Coping with Prejudice: 1 Peter in Social-Psychological Perspective* (Tübingen: Mohr Siebeck).

Horrell, David G. 2011. "'Race,' 'Nation,' 'People': Ethnic Identity-Construction in 1 Peter 2.9," *NTS* 58: 123–43.

Horrell, David G. 2016. "Ethnicisation, Marriage and Early Christian Identity: Critical Reflections on 1 Corinthians 7, 1 Peter 3 and Modern New Testament Scholarship," *NTS* 62: 439–60.

Howard, David M. 1994. "Rhetorical Criticism in Old Testament Studies," *BBR* 4: 87–104.

Hutcheon, Linda. 1985. *A Theory of Parody* (New York and London: Methuen).

Irigaray, Luce. 1991. *Marine Lover of Friedrich Nietzsche* (transl. Gillian Gill; Oxford: Oxford University Press).

Iser, Wolfgang. 1974. *The Implied Reader: Patterns of Communication in Prose Fiction from Bunyan to Beckett* (Baltimore: Johns Hopkins University Press).

Iser, Wolfgang. 1978. *The Act of Reading: A Theory of Aesthetic Response* (Baltimore: Johns Hopkins University Press).

Jager, Eric. 1993. *The Tempter's Voice: Language and the Fall in Medieval Literature* (Ithaca and London: Cornell University Press).

Jakobson, Roman. 1960. "Closing Statement: Linguistics and Poetics," in T. A. Sebeok (ed.), *Style in Language* (New York: Wiley): 350–77.

Jasper, David. 1990. "In the Sermon Which I Have Just Completed, Wherever I Said Aristotle, I Meant Saint Paul," in Martin Warner (ed.), *The Bible as Rhetoric: Studies in Biblical Persuasion and Credibility* (London: Routledge): 133–52.

Jeal, Roy. 2013. "Visual Interpretation: Blending Rhetorical Arts in Colossians 2.6–3.4," Unpublished paper delivered at the 2013 Annual SBL Meeting.

Jewett, Robert. 1986. *The Thessalonian Correspondence: Pauline Rhetoric and Millenarian Piety* (Philadelphia: Fortress).

Johnson-DeBaufre, Melanie and Laura S. Nasrallah. 2011. "Beyond the Heroic Paul: Toward a Feminist and Decolonizing Approach to the Letters of Paul," in Christopher Stanley (ed.), *The Colonized Apostle: Reading Paul through Postcolonial Eyes* (Minneapolis: Fortress): 161–74.

Kalmanofsky, Amy. 2008. *Terror All Around: The Rhetoric of Horror in the Book of Jeremiah* (LHBOTS 390; New York: T&T Clark).

Kaltner, John. 1999. "Is Daniel Also among the Prophets? The Rhetoric of Daniel 10–12," in Greg Carey and L. Gregory Bloomquist (eds.), *Vision and Persuasion: Rhetorical Dimensions of Apocalyptic Discourse* (St. Louis: Chalice): 41–60.

Kearns, Michael. 1999. *Rhetorical Narratology* (Lincoln: University of Nebraska).

Kennedy, George A. 1972. *The Art of Rhetoric in the Roman World* (Princeton: Princeton University Press).

Kennedy, George A. 1984. *New Testament Interpretation through Rhetorical Criticism* (Chapel Hill: University of North Carolina).

Kennedy, George A. 1994. *A New History of Classical Rhetoric* (Princeton: Princeton University Press).

King, Karen. 2013. "Rethinking the Diversity of Ancient Christianity: Responding to Suffering and Persecution," in Eduard Iricinschi, Lance Jenott, Nicola Denzey Lewis, and Philippa Townsend (eds.), *Beyond the Gnostic Gospels: Studies Building on the Work of Elaine Pagels* (Tübingen: Mohr Siebeck): 60–78.

Knight III, George W. 1991. "Husbands and Wives as Analogues of Christ and the Church," in Wayne Grudem and John Piper (eds.), *Recovering Biblical Manhood and Womanhood: A Response to Evangelical Feminism* (Wheaton, IL: Good News Publishers): 161–75.

Kolbet, Paul R. 2010. *Augustine and the Cure of Souls: Revising a Classical Ideal* (Notre Dame: University of Notre Dame Press).

Konstan, David. 2006. *The Emotions of the Ancient Greeks: Studies in Aristotle and Classical Literature* (Toronto: University of Toronto Press).

Kristeva, Julia. 1980. *Desire in Language: A Semiotic Approach to Literature and Art* (New York: Columbia University Press).

Kugel, James. 1981. *The Idea of Biblical Poetry: Parallelism and Its History*. (New Haven, CT: Yale University Press).

Lamb, Jonathan. 1995. *The Rhetoric of Suffering: Reading the Book of Job in the Eighteenth Century* (Oxford: Clarendon Press).

Lampe, Peter. 2010. "Rhetorical Analysis of Pauline Texts—Quo Vadit?," in J. Paul Sampley and Peter Lampe (eds.), *Paul and Rhetoric* (New York: T&T Clark): 3–21.

Langlands, Rebecca. 2015. "Roman Exemplarity: Mediating Between General and Particular," in Michele Lowrie and Susanne Lüdemann (eds.), *Exemplarity and Singularity: Thinking through Particulars in Philosophy, Literature, and Law* (New York: Routledge): 68–80.

Langlands, Rebecca. 2018. *Exemplary Ethics in Ancient Rome* (Cambridge: Cambridge University Press).

Lausberg, Heinrich. 1968. *Handbuch der literarischen Rhetorik. Eine Grundlegung der Literaturwissenschaft* (2 vols.; Munich: Heuber).

Le Roux, Elritia. 2019. "πονέμοντες τιμήν: 1 Peter as Subversive Text, Challenging Predominant Gender Roles in the 1st-Century Mediterranean World," *HTS Teologiese Studies/Theological Studies* 75 (4), a5430. https://doi.org/10.4102/hts.v75i4.5430.

Lee, Dorothy A. 1994. *The Symbolic Narratives of the Fourth Gospel: The Interplay of Form and Meaning* (Sheffield: Sheffield Academic).

Liebengood, Kelly D. 2014. *The Eschatology of 1 Peter: Considering the Influence of Zechariah 9–14* (Cambridge: Cambridge University Press).

Linafelt, Tod and Timothy K. Beal. 1998. "Introduction: In the Fray and at Risk," in Tod Linafelt and Timothy K. Beal (eds.), *God in the Fray: A Tribute to Walter Brueggemann* (Minneapolis: Augsburg): 1–10.

Lowth, Robert. 1753. *De sacra poesi Hebraeorum* (Oxford).

Luhmann, Niklas. 1989. *Ecological Communication* (trans. John Bednarz; Chicago: University of Chicago Press).

Lührmann, Dieter. 1980. "Neutestamentliche Haustafeln und antike Ökonomie," *NTS* 27: 83–97.

Lundbom, Jack R. 1997. *Jeremiah: A Study in Ancient Hebrew Rhetoric* (Winona Lake, IN: Eisenbrauns).

Lundbom, Jack R. 2013. *Biblical Rhetoric and Rhetorical Criticism* (Sheffield: Sheffield Phoenix).

MacDonald, Dennis R. 2001. *Mimesis and Intertextuality in Antiquity and Christianity* (Harrisburg: Trinity).

Mack, Burton. 1990. *Rhetoric and the New Testament* (Minneapolis: Fortress).

Mack, Burton and Vernon K. Robbins. 1989. *Patterns of Persuasion in the Gospels* (Sonoma, CA: Polebridge Press).

MacLuhan, Marshall. 1967. *Understanding Media: The Extensions of Man* (Bantam: New York).

Mailloux, Steven. 1989. *Rhetorical Power* (Ithaca, NY: Cornell University Press).

Malbon, Elizabeth Struthers. 2008. "Narrative Criticism: How Does the Story Mean?" in Anderson and Moore (eds.): 29–57.

Malherbe, Abraham J. 1986. *Moral Exhortation: A Greco-Roman Sourcebook* (Philadelphia: Westminster).

Malherbe, Abraham J. 1992. "Hellenistic Moralists and the New Testament," *ANRW* 2.26.1: 267–333.

Malina, Bruce and Jerome Neyrey. 1991. "Honor and Shame in Luke-Acts: Pivotal Values of the Mediterranean World," in Jerome Neyrey (ed.), *The Social World of Luke-Acts: Models for Interpretation* (Peabody, MA: Hendrickson): 25–65.

Marbury, Herbert. 2015. *Pillars of Cloud and Fire: The Politics of Exodus in African American Biblical Interpretation* (New York: New York University Press).

Marchal, Joseph. 2006. *Hierarchy, Unity, and Imitation: A Feminist Rhetorical Analysis of Power Dynamics in Paul's Letter to the Philippians* (Atlanta: SBL Press).

Marchal, Joseph. 2014. "Female Masculinity in Corinth? Bodily Citations and the Drag of History," *Neot* 48: 93–113.

Marrou, Henri Irénée. 1948. *Histoire de l'éducation dan l'antiquité* (Paris: Éditions du Seuil).

Martin, Michael W. and Bryan A. Nash. 2015. "Philippians 2:6–11 as Subversive *Hymnos*: A Study in the Light of Ancient Rhetorical Theory," *JTS* 66: 90–138.

Martin, Troy. 1990. *Metaphor and Composition in 1 Peter* (Atlanta: Scholars).

Martyn, Louis. 2003. *History and Theology in the Fourth Gospel* (Louisville: Westminster John Knox).

Matera, Frank. 2007. *New Testament Theology: Exploring Diversity and Unity* (Louisville: Westminster John Knox, 3rd ed.).

Maxwell, Kathy Reiko. 2010. *Hearing between the Lines: The Audience as Fellow-Worker in Luke-Acts and Its Literary Milieu* (New York: T&T Clark).

McGuire, Michael. 1982. "Some Problems with Rhetorical Example," *Pre/Text* 3: 121–36.

McKenzie, Steven L. and Stephen R. Haynes (eds.). 1999. *To Each Its Own Meaning: An Introduction to Biblical Criticisms and Their Application* (Louisville: Westminster John Knox).

Metzger, Bruce M. 1994. *A Textual Commentary on the Greek New Testament* (Stuttgart: Deutsche Bibelgesellschaft, 2nd ed.).

Meynet, Roland. 1990. "Histoire de l'analyse rhétorique en exégèse biblique," *Rhetorica* 8: 291–320.

Meynet, Roland. 1998. *Rhetorical Analysis: An Introduction to Biblical Rhetoric* (Sheffield: Sheffield Academic).

Michaels, J. Ramsey. 1988. *1 Peter* (WBC 49; Waco, TX: Word).

Miller, J. M., M. H. Prosser and T. W. Benson (eds.). 1973. *Readings in Medieval Rhetoric* (Bloomington: Indiana University Press).

Mitchell, Margaret. 1991. *Paul and the Rhetoric of Reconciliation: An Exegetical Investigation of the Language and Composition of 1 Corinthians* (Tübingen: Mohr Siebeck).

Moore, Stephen D. 1994. *Poststructuralism and the New Testament: Derrida and Foucault at the Foot of the Cross* (Minneapolis: Fortress).

Morgan, Teresa. 1998. *Literate Education in the Hellenistic and Roman Worlds* (Cambridge: Cambridge University Press).

Moxnes, Halvor. 2014. "The Beaten Body of Christ: Reading and Empowering Slave Bodies in 1 Peter," *Religion & Theology* 21: 125–41.

Muilenburg, James A. 1953. "A Study in Hebrew Rhetoric: Repetition and Style," *Vetus Testamentum Supplement* 1: 97–111.

Muilenburg, James A. 1969. "Form Criticism and Beyond," *JBL* 88: 1–18.

Muyumbu, Pascaline Nzosa and André Wénin. 2017. "Structure rhétorique de la prière d'Esther dans la LXX d'Esther (Suppl. C, 14b–30)," *Ephemerides Theologicae Lovanienses* 93: 289–311.

Nelevala, Surekha. 2007. "Jesus Asks the Samaritan Woman for a Drink: A Dalit Feminist Reading of John 4," *lectio difficilior: European Electronic Journal for Feminist Exegesis* (http://www.lectio.unibe.ch).

Newsom, Carol. 2014. "The Rhetoric of Jewish Apocalyptic Literature," in John J. Collins (ed.), *The Oxford Handbook of Apocalyptic Literature* (Oxford: Oxford University Press): 201–17.

Newsom, Carol. 2019. *Rhetoric and Hermeneutics: Approaches to Text, Tradition and Social Construction in Biblical and Second Temple Literature* (Tübingen: Mohr Siebeck).

Nietzsche, Friedrich. 1989. "Description of Ancient Rhetoric," in Sander Gilman, Carole Blair, and David J. Parent (eds., trans.), *Friedrich Nietzsche on Rhetoric and Language* (New York: Oxford University Press): 2–193.

Nussbaum, Martha. 1986. "Therapeutic Arguments: Epicurus and Aristotle," in Malcolm Schofield and Gisela Striker (eds.), *The Norms of Nature: Studies in Hellenistic Ethics* (New York: Cambridge University Press): 31–74.

Nussbaum, Martha. 1994. *The Therapy of Desire: Theory and Practice in Hellenistic Ethics* (Princeton: Princeton University Press).

O'Day, Gail R. 1986. "Narrative Mode and Theological Claim: A Study in the Fourth Gospel," *JBL* 105: 657–68.

O'Leary, Stephen D. 1991. *Arguing the Apocalypse: A Theory of Millennial Rhetoric* (New York: Praeger).

Okure, Teresa. 1988. *The Johannine Approach to Mission: A Contextual Study of John 4.1–42* (Tübingen: J. C. B. Mohr).

Olbricht, Thomas H. and Jerry L. Sumney (eds.). 2001. *Paul and Pathos* (Atlanta: SBL Press).

Olender, Maurice. 1992. *The Languages of Paradise: Race, Religion, and Philology in the Nineteenth Century* (Cambridge, MA: Harvard University Press).

Otto, Rudolf. 1923; 2nd ed., 1950. *The Idea of the Holy* (trans. John W. Harvey; Oxford: Oxford University Press [*Das Heilige*, 1917]).

Overbeck, Franz. 1882. "Über die Anfänge der patristischen Literatur," *Hist. Zeitschr.* 48: 412–72.

Parsons, Mikeal and Michael Wade Martin. 2018. *Ancient Rhetoric and the New Testament: The Influence of Elementary Greek Composition* (Waco, TX: Baylor University Press).

Penner, Todd and Davina C. 2012. "Rhetorical Approaches: Introducing the Art of Persuasion in Paul and Pauline Studies," in Joseph A. Marchal (ed.), *Studying Paul's Letters: Contemporary Perspectives and Methods* (Minneapolis: Fortress): 33–52.

Perelman, Chaim and Lucie Olbrechts-Tyteca. 1969. *The New Rhetoric: A Treatise on Argumentation* (trans. John Wilkinson and Purcell Weaver; Notre Dame: University of Notre Dame Press).

Perkins, Judith. 1995. *The Suffering Self: Pain and Narrative Representation in the Early Christian Era* (New York: Routledge).

Pernot, Laurent. 2005. *Rhetoric in Antiquity* (trans. W. E. Higgins; Washington, DC: Catholic University of America Press).

Perry, Menakhem. 1979. "Literary Dynamics: How the Order of a Text Creates Its Meanings [With an Analysis of Faulkner's 'A Rose for Emily']," *Poetics Today* 1: 35–64, 311–61.

Petitfils, James. 2016. *Mos Christianorum: The Moral Discourse of Exemplarity and the Jewish and Christian Language of Leadership* (Tübingen: Mohr Siebeck).

Phelan, James. 1996. *Narrative as Rhetoric: Technique, Audiences, Ethics, Ideology* (Columbus, OH: Ohio State University Press).

Phelan, James. 2007. "Rhetoric/Ethics," in David Herman (ed.), *The Cambridge Companion to Narrative* (Cambridge: Cambridge University Press): 209–16.

Pire, François. 1980. "Rhetoric and Rhetorics," *Philosophy & Rhetoric* 13: 147–49.

Pokorný, Petr. 1991. *Colossians* (Peabody: Hendrickson).

Poland, Lynn. 1990. "The Bible and the Rhetorical Sublime," in Martin Warner (ed.), *The Bible as Rhetoric: Studies in Biblical Persuasion and Credibility* (London: Routledge): 29–50.

Porter, Stanley (ed.). 2001. *Handbook of Classical Rhetoric in the Hellenistic Period* (Leiden: Brill).

Porter, Stanley. 2013. "Hellenistic Oratory and Paul of Tarsus," in Christos Kremmydas and Kathryn Tempest (eds.), *Hellenistic Oratory: Continuity and Change* (Oxford: Oxford University Press): 319–60.

Porter, Stanley. 2017. "Rhetoric and New Testament Studies," in Michael J. MacDonald (ed.), *The Oxford Handbook of Rhetorical Studies* (Oxford: Oxford University Press): 649–60.

Powell, Mark Allen. 1993. "Expected and Unexpected Readings of Matthew: What the Reader Knows," *Asbury Theological Journal* 48: 41–51.

Powery, Emerson and Rodney Sadler, Jr. 2016. *The Genesis of Liberation: Biblical Interpretation in the Antebellum Narratives of the Enslaved* (Louisville: Westminster/ John Knox).

Price, Bennett J. 1975. "Paradeigma and Exemplum in Ancient Rhetorical Theory." PhD dissertation, University of California at Berkeley.

Rabbow, Paul. 1954. *Seelenführung: Methodik Der Exerzitien in Der Antike* (München: Kösel Verlag).

Rabinowitz, Peter. 1987. *Before Reading: Narrative Conventions and the Politics of Interpretation* (New York: Cornell University Press).

Regev, Eyal. 2007. *Sectarianism in Qumran: A Cross-Cultural Perspective* (Berlin: de Gruyter).

Reicke, Bo. 1964. *The Epistles of James, Peter, and Jude* (AB 37; New York: Doubleday).

Reinhartz, Adele. 2018. *Cast Out of the Covenant: Jews and Anti-Judaism in the Gospel of John* (Lanham: Lexington Books: Fortress Academic).

Renan, Ernest. 1888. *History of the People of Israel till the Time of King David, vol. 1 of History of the People of Israel* (trans. C. B. Pitman and D. Bingham; London: Chapman and Hall).

Resseguie, James. 2001. *The Strange Gospel: Narrative Design and Point of View in John* (Leiden: Brill).

Rhoads, David M. 2004. *Reading Mark, Engaging the Gospel* (Minneapolis: Fortress).

Richards, Ivor Armstrong. 1936. *The Philosophy of Rhetoric* (Oxford: Oxford University Press).

Robbins, Vernon K. 1991. "Writing as a Rhetorical Act in Plutarch and the Gospels," in Duane F. Watson (ed.), *Persuasive Artistry: Studies in New Testament Rhetoric in Honor of George A. Kennedy* (Sheffield: Sheffield Academic): 57–86.

Robbins, Vernon K. 1996. *The Tapestry of Early Christian Discourse: Rhetoric, Society and Ideology* (London: Routledge).

Robbins, Vernon K. 2002. "The Rhetorical Full-Turn in Biblical Interpretation: Reconfiguring Rhetorical-Political Analysis," in Stanley E. Porter and Dennis L. Stamps (eds.), *Rhetorical Criticism and the Bible* (Sheffield: Sheffield Academic): 48–60.

Robbins, Vernon K. 2008. "Rhetography: A New Way of Seeing the Familiar Text," in C. Clifton Black and Duane F. Watson (eds.), *Words Well Spoken: George Kennedy's Rhetoric of the New Testament* (Waco, TX: Baylor University Press): 81–106.

Roller, Matthew. 2004. "Exemplarity in Roman Culture: The Cases of Horatius Codes and Cloelia," *Classical Philology* 99: 1–56.

Roller, Matthew. 2018. *Models from the Past in Roman Culture: A World of Exempla* (Cambridge: Cambridge University Press).

Ronsse, Erin. 2006. "Rhetoric of Martyrs: Listening to Saints Perpetua and Felicitas," *JECS* 14: 283–327.

Runesson, Anna. 2007. *Exegesis in the Making: Postcolonialism and New Testament Studies* (BINS 103; Leiden: Brill).

Rylaardsam, David. 2014. *Imitating Divine Pedagogy: The Coherence of John Chrysostom's Theology and Preaching* (Oxford: Oxford University Press).

Sanders, James A. 1955. *Suffering as Divine Discipline in the Old Testament and Post-Biblical Judaism* (Rochester, NY: Colgate Rochester Divinity School).

Sargent, Benjamin. 2015. *Written to Serve: The Use of Scripture in 1 Peter* (London: T&T Clark).

Schertz, Mary H. 1992. "Nonretaliation and the Haustafeln in 1 Peter," in W. H. Swartley (ed.), *The Love of Enemy and Nonretaliation in the New Testament* (Louisville: Westminster/John Knox): 258–86.

Schmidt, Karl Ludwig. 1923. "Die Stellung der Evangelien in der allgemeinen Literaturgeschichte," in H. Schmidt (ed.), *Eucharisterion: Hermann Gunkel zum 60. Gebrutstag* (Göttingen: Vandenhoeck & Ruprecht): 50–134.

Schnackenburg, Rudolf. 1968. *The Gospel according to St. John, Vol. I* (New York: Crossroad).

Schneider, Tammi J. 2004. *Sarah: Mother of Nations* (New York: Continuum).

Schneider, Tammi J. 2008. *Mothers of Promise: Women in the Book of Genesis* (Grand Rapids: Baker Academic).

Schneiders, Sandra Marie. 1999. *The Revelatory Text: Interpreting the New Testament as Sacred Scripture* (Collegeville, MN: Liturgical Press, 2nd ed.).

Schöttgen, Christian. 1733. *Horae Hebraicae et Talmudicae I* (Leipzig).

Schroeder, David. 1959. *Die Haustafeln des neuen Testaments* (*inhre Herkunft und theologishcher Sinn*) (Diss. Hamburg).

Schüssler Fiorenza, Elisabeth. 1984. *Bread Not Stone: The Challenge of Feminist Biblical Interpretation* (Boston: Beacon).

Schüssler Fiorenza, Elisabeth. 1988. "The Ethics of Biblical Interpretation: Decentering Biblical Scholarship," *JBL* 107: 3–17.

Schüssler Fiorenza, Elisabeth. 1992. *But She Said: Feminist Practices of Biblical Interpretation* (Boston: Beacon Press).

Schüssler Fiorenza, Elisabeth. 1996. "Challenging the Rhetorical Half-Turn: Feminist and Rhetorical Biblical Criticism," in Stanley E. Porter and Thomas H. Olbricht (eds.), *Rhetoric, Scripture, and Theology: Essays from the 1994 Pretoria Conference* (Sheffield: Sheffield Academic): 28–53.

Schüssler Fiorenza, Elisabeth. 1999. *Rhetoric and Ethic: The Politics of Biblical Studies* (Minneapolis: Fortress).

Schüssler Fiorenza, Elisabeth. 2007. *The Power of the Word: Scripture and the Rhetoric of Empire* (Minneapolis: Fortress).

Schüssler Fiorenza, Elisabeth. 2017. *1 Peter: An Introduction and Study Guide: Reading against the Grain* (London: T&T Clark).

Schutter, William. 1989. *Hermeneutic and Composition in 1 Peter* (WUNT; Tübingen: Mohr Siebeck).

Selby, Gary. 2016. *Not with Wisdom of Words: Nonrational Persuasion in the New Testament* (Grand Rapids: Eerdmans).

Shakespeare, William. 1992. *The Merchant of Venice* (New York: Washington Square Press).

Sharp, Carolyn. 2009. *Irony and Meaning in the Hebrew Bible* (Bloomington: Indiana University Press).

Sharp, Carolyn. 2015. "Wrestling the Word: Submission and Resistance as Holy Hermeneutical Acts," *Anglican Theological Review* 97: 5–18.

Siegert, Folker. 1985. *Argumentation bei Paulus: Gezeigt an Rom 9–11* (Tübingen: Mohr Siebeck).

Sly, Dorothy. 1991. "1 Peter 3:6b in the Light of Philo and Josephus," *JBL* 110: 126–29.

Stamps, Dennis L. 1997. "Rhetorical and Narratological Criticism," in Stanley E. Porter (ed.), *Handbook to Exegesis of the New Testament* (Leiden: Brill): 219–39.

Sternberg, Meir. 1985. *The Poetics of Biblical Narrative* (Bloomington: Indiana University Press).

Stowers, Stanley. 1981. *The Diatribe and Paul's Letter to the Romans* (Chico, CA: Scholars).

Stowers, Stanley. 1984. *A Rereading of Romans: Justice, Jews and Gentiles* (New Haven, CT: Yale University Press).

Sugirtharajah, R. S. (ed.). 2005. *The Postcolonial Biblical Reader* (Oxford: Blackwell Publishing).

Talbert, Charles. 1991. *Learning through Suffering: The Educational Value of Suffering in the New Testament and in Its Milieu* (Collegeville, MN: Liturgical Press).

Tannehill, Robert C. 1986. *The Narrative Unity of Luke-Acts: A Literary Interpretation* (2 vols.; Philadelphia: Fortress).

Thompson, Thomas L. and Philippe Wajdenbaum (eds.). 2014. *The Bible and Hellenism: Greek Influence on Jewish and Early Christian Literature* (London: Acumen).

Thompson, Thomas L. 2018. "'Rewritten Bible' or Reiterative Rhetoric: Examples from Yahweh's Garden," in Jesper Høgenhaven, Jesper Tang Nielsen, and Heike Omerzu (eds.), *Rewriting and Reception in and of the Bible* (Tübingen: Mohr Siebeck): 49–63.

Thorsteinsson, Runar. 2010. *Roman Christianity and Roman Stoicism* (Oxford: Oxford University Press).

Tolmie, D. François. 2005. *Persuading the Galatians: A Text-Centred Rhetorical Analysis of a Pauline Letter* (Tübingen: Mohr Siebeck).

Too, Yun Lee and Niall Livingstone (eds.). 1998. *Pedagogy and Power: Rhetorics of Classical Learning* (Cambridge: Cambridge University Press).

Too, Yun Lee. 2000. *The Pedagogical Contract: The Economies of Teaching and Learning in the Ancient World* (Ann Arbor: University of Michigan Press).

Too, Yun Lee (ed.). 2001. *Education in Greek and Roman Antiquity* (Leiden: Brill).

Trebilco, Paul. 2004. *The Early Christians in Ephesus from Paul to Ignatius* (Tübingen: Mohr Siebeck).

Trible, Phyllis. 1994. *Rhetorical Criticism: Context, Method, and the Book of Jonah* (Minneapolis: Fortress).

Tull, Patricia. 1999. "Rhetorical Criticism and Intertextuality," in McKenzie and Haynes (eds.): 156–80.

VanderKam, James. 1996. *The Jewish Apocalyptic Heritage in Early Christianity* (Minneapolis: Fortress).

Vatz, Richard. 1973. "The Myth of the Rhetorical Situation," *Philosophy and Rhetoric* 6: 154–61.

Vayntrub, Jacqueline. 2019. *Beyond Orality: Performance and the Composition of Biblical Poetry* (New York: Routledge).

Visser, Jacobie M. Helena. 2017. "Following the Man on the Slippery Slide: Christ in 1 Peter," *Neot* 51: 337–57.

Walker, Jeffrey and Thomas Benson. 2012. *The Genuine Teachers of This Art: Rhetorical Education in Antiquity* (Columbia, SC: University of South Carolina Press).

Ward, John O. 2019. *Classical Rhetoric in the Middle Ages: The Medieval Rhetors and Their Art 400–1300, with Manuscript Survey to 1500 CE* (Leiden: Brill).

Watson, Duane F. 1988. "Rhetorical Criticism," in Geoffrey W. Bromily (ed.), *International Standard Bible Encyclopedia* (4 vols; Grand Rapids: Eerdmans): 4: 181–82.

Watson, Duane F. and Alan J. Hauser. 1994. *Rhetorical Criticism of the Bible: A Comprehensive Bibliography with Notes on History and Method* (Leiden: Brill).

Watson, Duane F. 2006. *The Rhetoric of the New Testament: A Bibliographic Survey* (Blandford: Deo).

Webb, Robert. 2007. "Intertexture and Rhetorical Strategy in First Peter's Apocalyptic Discourse: A Study in Sociorhetorical Interpretation," in Robert Webb and Betsy Bauman-Martin (eds.), *Reading First Peter with New Eyes: Methodological Reassessments of the Letter of First Peter* (New York: T&T Clark): 72–110.

Weidinger, Karl. 1926. *Die Haustafeln, ein Stuch urchristlicher Paraenese* (Leipzig: Hinrichs).

Welch, Kathleen. 1990. *The Contemporary Reception of Classical Rhetoric: Appropriations of Ancient Discourse* (Hillsdale, NJ: Lawrence Erlbaum).

Wilder, Amos. 1956. "Scholars, Theologians, and Ancient Rhetoric," *JBL* 75: 1–11.

Wilder, Amos. 1971. *Early Christian Rhetoric: The Language of the Gospel* (Cambridge, MA: Harvard University Press).

Williams, Travis B. 2012. *Persecution in 1 Peter: Differentiating and Contextualizing Early Christian Suffering* (Leiden: Brill).

Williams, Travis B. 2014. "The Divinity and Humanity of Caesar in 1Peter 2,13: Early Christian Resistance to the Emperor and His Cult," *ZNW* 105: 131–47.

Wire, Antoinette Clark. 1990. *The Corinthian Women Prophets: A Reconstruction through Paul's Rhetoric* (Minneapolis: Fortress).

Witherington III, Benjamin. 2009. *New Testament Rhetoric: An Introductory Guide to the Art of Persuasion in and of the New Testament* (Eugene, OR: Cascade Books).

Wolterstorff, Nicholas. 2002. "The Silence of the God Who Speaks," in Daniel Howard-Snyder and Paul K. Moser (eds)., *Divine Hiddenness of God*, ed. Daniel Howard-Snyder and Paul K. Moser (Cambridge: Cambridge University Press); 215–28.

Wuellner, Wilhelm. 1987. "Where Is Rhetorical Criticism Taking Us?," *CBQ* 49: 448–63.

Wuellner, Wilhelm. 1991. "Rhetorical Criticism and Its Theory in Culture-Critical Perspective: The Narrative Rhetoric of John 11," in P. J. Hartin and J. H. Petzer (eds.), *Text and Interpretation: New Approaches in the Criticism of the New Testament* (Leiden: Brill): 167–81.

Zaeske, Susan. 2000. "Unveiling Esther as a Pragmatic Radical Rhetoric," *Philosophy and Rhetoric* 33: 193–220.

Zimmermann, Mirjam and Ruben. 1998. "Brautwerbung in Samarien? Von der moralischen zur metaphorischen Interpretation von Joh 4," *ZNT* 1: 40–50.

Zimmermann, Ruben. 2014. "From a Jewish Man to the Savior of the World: Narrative and Symbols Forming a Step by Step Christology in John 4,1–42," in Joseph Verheyden, Geert van Oyen, Michael Labahn, Reimund Bieringer (eds.), *Studies in the Gospel of John and Its Christology* (Leuven: Peeters): 99–118.

Zulick, Margaret D. 2009. "Rhetoric of Religion: A Map of the Territory," in Andrea Lunsford, Kirt Wilson, and Rosa Eberly (eds.), *The SAGE Handbook of Rhetorical Studies* (Los Angeles: SAGE): 125–39.

Zulick, Margaret D. 1992. "The Active Force of Hearing: The Ancient Hebrew Language of Persuasion," *Rhetorica* 10: 367–80.